Acoustic & Digital

PIANO BUYER®

MODEL & PRICE SUPPLEMENT

Spring 2019

LARRY FINE
Editor

WWW.PIANOBUYER.COM

Piano Buyer Model & Price Supplement is published by:

Brookside Press LLC
P.O. Box 601041
San Diego, CA 92160 USA

619.738.4155
619.810.0425 (fax)
info@pianobuyer.com
www.pianobuyer.com

Piano Buyer Model & Price Supplement / Spring 2019
copyright © 2019 by Brookside Press LLC.
All rights reserved.
"The Piano Book" is a Registered Trademark of Lawrence Fine.
"Piano Buyer" is a Registered Trademark of Brookside Press LLC.

ISBN 978-1-92914570-6

Distributed to the book trade by Independent Publishers Group,
814 North Franklin St., Chicago, IL 60610
(800) 888-4741 or (312) 337-0747
www.ipgbook.com

Reasonable efforts have been made to secure accurate information for this publication. Due in part to the fact that manufacturers and distributors will not always willingly make this information available, however, some indirect sources have been relied on.

Neither the editors nor publisher make any guarantees with respect to the accuracy of the information contained herein, and will not be liable for damages—incidental, consequential, or otherwise—resulting from the use of the information.

CONTENTS

Acoustic Piano
Model & Pricing Guide

This guide contains price information for nearly every brand, model, style, and finish of new piano that has regular distribution in the United States and, for the most part, Canada. Omitted are some marginal, local, or "stencil" brands (brands sold only by a single dealership). Prices are in U.S. dollars and are subject to change. Prices include an allowance for the approximate cost of freight from the U.S. warehouse to the dealer, and for a minimal amount of make-ready by the dealer. The prices cited in this edition were compiled in February 2019 and apply only to piano sales in the U.S. Prices in Canada are often very different due to differences in duty, freight, sales practices, and competition.

Note that the prices of European pianos vary with the value of the dollar against the euro. For this edition, the exchange rate used by most manufacturers was approximately €1 = $1.15. Prices of European pianos include import duties and estimated costs of airfreight (where applicable) to the dealer. However, actual costs will vary depending on the shipping method used, the port of entry, and other variables. Also keep in mind that the dealer may have purchased the piano at an exchange rate different from the current one.

Unless otherwise indicated, cabinet styles are assumed to be traditional in nature, with minimal embellishment and straight legs. Recognizable furniture styles are noted, and the manufacturer's own trademarked style name is used when an appropriate generic name could not be determined. Please see the section on "Furniture Style and Finish" in our online article "**Piano-Buying Basics**" for descriptions or definitions of terms relating to style and finish.

"Size" refers to the height of a vertical or the length of a grand. These are the only dimensions that vary significantly and relate to the quality of the instrument. The height of a vertical piano is measured from the floor to the top of the piano. The length of a grand piano is measured from the very front (keyboard end) to the very back (tail end) with the lid closed.

About Prices

The subject of piano pricing is difficult, complicated, and controversial. One of the major problems is that piano dealers tend to prefer that list prices be as high as possible so they can still make a profit while appearing to give very generous discounts. Honesty about pricing is resisted.

But even knowing what is "honest" is a slippery business because many factors can have a dramatic effect on piano pricing. For one thing, different dealerships can pay very different wholesale prices for the same merchandise, depending on:

- the size of the dealership and how many pianos it agrees to purchase at one time or over a period of time
- whether the dealer pays cash or finances the purchase
- the degree to which the dealer buys manufacturer overstocks at bargain prices
- any special terms the dealership negotiates with the manufacturer or distributor.

In addition to these variations at the wholesale level, retail conditions also vary from dealer to dealer or from one geographic area to another, including:

- the general cost of doing business in the dealer's area
- the level of pre- and post-sale service the dealer provides
- the level of professionalism of the sales staff and the degree to which they are trained and compensated
- the ease of local comparison shopping by the consumer for a particular type of piano or at a particular price level.

Besides the variations between dealerships, the circumstances of each sale at any particular dealership can vary tremendously due to such things as:

- how long a particular piano has been sitting around unsold, racking up finance charges for the dealer
- the dealer's financial condition and need for cash at the moment
- competing sales events going on at other dealerships in the area
- whether or not the customer is trading in a used piano.

As difficult as it might be to come up with accurate price information, confusion and ignorance about pricing for such a high-ticket item is intolerable to the consumer, and can cause decision-making paralysis. I strongly believe that a reasonable amount of price information actually greases the wheels of commerce by giving the customer the peace of mind that allows him or her to make a purchase. In this guide I've tried to give a level of information about price that reasonably respects the interests of both buyer and seller, given the range of prices that can exist for any particular model.

Prices include a bench except where noted. (Even where a price doesn't include a bench, the dealer will almost always provide one and quote a price that includes it.) Most dealers will also include delivery and one or two tunings in the home, but these are optional and a matter of agreement between you and the dealer. Prices do not include sales tax.

In this guide, two prices are given for each model: Manufacturer's Suggested Retail Price (MSRP) and Suggested Maximum Price (SMP).

Manufacturer's Suggested Retail Price (MSRP)
The MSRP is a price provided by the manufacturer or distributor and designed as a starting point from which dealers are expected to discount. I include it here for reference purposes—only rarely does a customer pay this price. The MSRP is usually

figured as a multiple of the wholesale price, but the specific multiple used differs from company to company. **For that reason, it's fruitless to compare prices of different brands by comparing discounts from the MSRP.** To see why, consider the following scenario:

Manufacturer A sells brand A through its dealer A. The wholesale price to the dealer is $1,000, but for the purpose of setting the MSRP, the manufacturer doubles the wholesale price and sets the MSRP at $2,000. Dealer A offers a 25 percent discount off the MSRP, for a "street price" of $1,500.

Manufacturer B sells brand B through its dealer B. The wholesale price to the dealer is also $1,000, but manufacturer B triples the wholesale price and sets the MSRP at $3,000. Dealer B offers a generous 50 percent discount, for a street price of, again, $1,500.

Although the street price is the same for both pianos, a customer shopping at both stores and knowing nothing about the wholesale price or how the MSRPs are computed, is likely to come away with the impression that brand B, with a discount of 50 percent off $3,000, is a more "valuable" piano and a better deal than brand A, with a discount of 25 percent off $2,000. Other factors aside, which dealer do you think will get the sale? It's important to note that there is nothing about brand B that makes it deserving of a higher MSRP than brand A—how to compute the MSRP is essentially a marketing decision on the part of the manufacturer.

Because of the deceptive manner in which MSRPs are so often used, some manufacturers no longer provide them. In those cases, I've left the MSRP column blank.

Suggested Maximum Price (SMP)

The Suggested Maximum Price (SMP) is a price I've created, based on a profit margin that I've uniformly applied to published wholesale prices. (Where the published wholesale price is unavailable, or is believed to be bogus, which is sometimes the case, I've made a reasonable attempt to estimate the SMP from other sources.) Because in the SMP, unlike in the MSRP, the same profit margin is applied to all brands, the SMP can be used as a "benchmark" price for the purpose of comparing brands and offers. The specific profit margin I've chosen for the SMP is one that dealers often try—but rarely manage—to attain. Also included in the SMP, in most cases, are allowances for duty (where applicable), freight charges, and a minimal amount of make-ready by the dealer. Although the SMP is my creation, it's a reasonable estimate of the **maximum** price you should realistically expect to pay. However, **most sales actually take place at a discount to the SMP**, as discussed below.

Actual Selling or "Street" Price

As you should know by now from reading this publication, most dealers of new pianos are willing—and expect—to negotiate. Only a handful of dealers have non-negotiable prices. For more information on negotiating, please see "**Negotiating Price and Trade-Ins**" in our online article "Piano Buying Basics." *The Piano Book* also gives advice about negotiating tactics.

How good a deal you can negotiate will vary, depending on the many factors listed earlier. But in order to make a budget, or to know which pianos are within your budget, or just to feel comfortable enough to actually make a purchase, you need some idea of what is considered normal in the industry. In most cases, discounts from the Suggested Maximum Price range from 15 to 25 percent. This does *not* mean that if you try hard enough, you can talk the salesperson into giving you a 25 percent discount. Rather, it reflects the wide range of prices possible in the marketplace due to the many factors discussed earlier. For budgeting purposes only, I suggest figuring a discount of about 20 percent. This will probably bring you within about 5 percent, one way or the other, of the final negotiated price. Important exception: Discounts on Steinway pianos generally range from 0 to 10 percent. For your convenience in figuring the effects of various discounts, a discount calculator is included in the model and price database, accessible through our website.

There is no single "fair" or "right" price that can be applied to every purchase. The only fair price is that which the buyer and seller agree on. It's understandable that you would like to pay as little as possible, but remember that piano shopping is not just about chasing the lowest price. Be sure you are getting the instrument that best suits your needs and preferences, and that the dealer is committed to providing the appropriate level of pre- and post-sale service.

Searchable Database

To search piano models by price range, size, quality level, furniture style, finish, and more, please go to **www.pianobuyer.com** to access the free searchable database of acoustic piano models and prices.

Model	Feet	Inches	Description	MSRP	SMP

BALDWIN
Verticals

Model	Feet	Inches	Description	MSRP	SMP
B342		43	French Provincial Satin Cherry	10,545	7,590
B442		43	Satin Mahogany	10,545	7,590
BP1		47	Polished Ebony	9,265	6,790
BP1/S		47	Polished Ebony with Silver Hardware	9,595	6,996
B243		47	Satin Ebony/Walnut (school piano)	10,545	7,590
BP3		48	French Provincial Polished Rosewood	10,865	7,790
BP3T		48	Polished Ebony	10,545	7,590
BP3T		48	Polished Rosewood	10,865	7,790
BP5		49	Polished Ebony	11,185	7,990
BP5		49	Polished Rosewood	11,505	8,190
B252		52	Satin Ebony	14,065	9,390

Grands

Model	Feet	Inches	Description	MSRP	SMP
BP148	4	10	Satin Ebony Lacquer	24,945	16,590
BP148	4	10	Polished Ebony	21,425	14,390
BP148	4	10	Polished Ebony with Silver Hardware	22,395	14,990
BP148	4	10	Polished Mahogany/Walnut/White	22,395	14,990
BP152	5		Satin Ebony Lacquer	27,825	18,390
BP152	5		Polished Ebony	24,325	16,190
BP152	5		Polished Mahogany/Walnut/White	25,295	16,790
BP165	5	5	Satin Ebony Lacquer	29,995	19,790
BP165	5	5	Polished Ebony	26,595	17,590
BP165	5	5	Polished Ebony with Silver Hardware	27,550	18,190
BP165	5	5	Polished Mahogany/Walnut/White	27,550	18,190
BP178	5	10	Satin Ebony Lacquer	39,995	25,990
BP178	5	10	Polished Ebony	35,825	23,390
BP178	5	10	Polished Mahogany/Walnut	37,425	24,390
BP190	6	3	Satin Ebony Lacquer	47,345	30,590
BP190	6	3	Polished Ebony	42,895	27,790
BP190	6	3	Polished Mahogany/Walnut	44,795	28,990
BP211	6	11	Polished Ebony	63,995	40,990

BECHSTEIN, C.
C. Bechstein Academy Series Verticals

Model	Feet	Inches	Description	MSRP	SMP
A114 Modern		44	Polished Ebony	24,280	23,848
A112 Modern		44	Polished White	26,220	26,220
A114 Chrome Art		44	Polished Ebony	26,220	26,220
A112 Chrome Art		44	Polished White	28,180	28,180
A114 Compact		45.5	Polished Ebony	26,220	26,180
A116 Compact		45.5	Polished White	28,180	28,180
A116 Compact		45.5	Satin and Polished Walnut/Mahogany/Cherry	29,140	29,140
A124 Imposant		49	Polished Ebony	28,180	28,180
A124 Imposant		49	Polished White	30,120	30,120
A124 Style		49.5	Polished Ebony	28,180	28,180

Acoustic Piano Model & Pricing Guide

5

Model	Feet	Inches	Description	MSRP	SMP
BECHSTEIN, C. *(continued)*					
A124 Style		49.5	Polished White	30,120	30,120
A124 Style		49.5	Satin and Polished Mahogany/Walnut/Cherry	32,060	32,060
C. Bechstein Verticals					
Millenium 116K		46	Polished Ebony	30,120	30,120
Millenium 116K		46	Polished White	32,060	32,060
Classic 118		46.5	Polished Ebony	32,060	32,060
Classic 118		46.5	Polished White	34,000	34,000
Classic 118		46.5	Satin and Polished Walnut/Mahogany/Cherry	35,960	35,960
Contour 118		46.5	Polished Ebony	32,060	32,060
Contour 118		46.5	Polished White	34,000	34,000
Contour 118		46.5	Satin and Polished Walnut/Mahogany/Cherry	35,960	35,960
Classic 124		49	Polished Ebony	39,840	39,840
Classic 124		49	Polished White	41,780	41,780
Classic 124		49	Satin and Polished Walnut/Mahogany/Cherry	43,720	43,720
Elegance 124		49	Polished Ebony	39,840	39,840
Elegance 124		49	Polished White	41,780	41,780
Elegance 124		49	Satin and Polished Walnut/Mahogany/Cherry		
Concert 8		51.5	Polished Ebony	68,980	68,980
Concert 8		51.5	Polished White	70,860	70,860
Concert 8		51.5	Polished Walnut/Mahogany		
Concert 8		51.5	Polished Burl Walnut		
Concert 8		51.5	Polished Cherry w/Inlays		
C. Bechstein Academy Series Grands					
A160	5	3	Polished Ebony	65,620	65,620
A160	5	3	Satin and Polished Mahogany/Walnut	79,240	79,240
A160	5	3	Polished White	69,520	69,520
A175	5	9	Polished Ebony	69,520	69,520
A175	5	9	Satin and Polished Walnut/Mahogany	83,120	83,120
A175	5	9	Polished White	75,340	75,340
A190	6	3	Polished Ebony	73,400	73,400
A190	6	3	Satin and Polished Mahogany/Walnut	87,020	87,020
A190	6	3	Polished White	79,240	79,240
A208	6	8	Polished Ebony	85,060	84,182
A208	6	8	Satin and Polished Mahogany/Walnut	104,520	102,472
A208	6	8	Polished White	90,900	90,900
A228	7	5	Polished Ebony	98,680	95,458
A228	7	5	Satin and Polished Mahogany/Walnut	118,120	118,120
A228	7	5	Polished White	104,520	104,520
C. Bechstein Grands					
L167	5	6	Polished Ebony	126,040	120,446
L167	5	6	Satin and Polished Mahogany/Walnut/Cherry	144,920	142,100
L167	5	6	Polished White	131,700	131,700
M/P192	6	4	Polished Ebony	148,700	139,538
M/P192	6	4	Satin and Polished Mahogany/Walnut/Cherry	167,580	162,070
M/P192	6	4	Polished White	158,140	158,140

Model	Feet	Inches	Description	MSRP	SMP
BECHSTEIN, C. *(continued)*					
B212	6	11	Polished Ebony	171,360	171,360
B212	6	11	Polished White	180,800	180,800
C234	7	7	Polished Ebony	209,140	209,140
C234	7	7	Polished White	220,480	220,480
D282	9	2	Polished Ebony	272,240	268,372
D282	9	2	Polished White	287,340	287,340

BLÜTHNER

Prices do not include bench.

Verticals

Model	Feet	Inches	Description	MSRP	SMP
D		45	Satin and Polished Ebony	34,648	32,356
D		45	Satin and Polished Walnut/Mahogany	37,420	34,864
D		45	Satin and Polished Cherry	37,594	35,022
D		45	Satin and Polished White	37,074	34,551
D		45	Satin and Polished Bubinga/Yew/Rosewood/Macassar	38,460	35,805
C		46	Satin and Polished Ebony	38,498	35,840
C		46	Satin and Polished Mahogany/Walnut	41,578	38,627
C		46	Satin and Polished Cherry	41,771	38,802
C		46	Satin and Polished White	41,193	38,279
C		46	Satin and Polished Bubinga/Yew/Rosewood/Macassar	42,733	39,672
C		46	Saxony Polished Pyramid Mahogany	48,893	45,247
C		46	Polished Burl Walnut/Camphor	51,973	48,034
A		49	Satin and Polished Ebony	44,357	41,142
A		49	Satin and Polished Mahogany/Walnut	47,905	44,353
A		49	Satin and Polished Cherry	48,127	44,554
A		49	Satin and Polished White	47,462	43,952
A		49	Satin and Polished Bubinga/Yew/Rosewood/Macassar	49,236	45,557
A		49	Saxony Polished Pyramid Mahogany	56,333	51,980
A		49	Polished Burl Walnut/Camphor	59,882	55,192
B		52	Satin and Polished Ebony	50,215	46,443
B		52	Satin and Polished Mahogany/Walnut	54,232	50,079
B		52	Satin and Polished Cherry	54,483	50,306
B		52	Satin and Polished White	53,730	49,624
B		52	Satin and Polished Bubinga/Yew/Rosewood/Macassar	55,739	51,443
B		52	Saxony Polished Pyramid Mahogany	63,773	58,713
B		52	Polished Burl Walnut/Camphor	67,790	62,348
S		57.5	Satin and Polished Ebony	67,479	62,067
S		57.5	Satin and Polished Mahogany/Walnut	72,878	66,953
S		57.5	Satin and Polished Cherry	73,215	67,258
S		57.5	Satin and Polished White	72,203	66,342
S		57.5	Satin and Polished Bubinga/Yew/Rosewood/Macassar	74,902	68,785
S		57.5	Saxony Polished Pyramid Mahogany	85,699	78,556
S		57.5	Polished Burl Walnut/Camphor	91,097	83,441
Verticals			e-volution Hybrid Piano System, add	8,200	7,421
Verticals			Sostenuto, add	3,400	3,077

Model	Feet	Inches	Description	MSRP	SMP
BLÜTHNER *(continued)*					
Grands					
11	5	1	Satin and Polished Ebony	86,874	79,619
11	5	1	Satin and Polished Mahogany/Walnut	93,824	85,909
11	5	1	Satin and Polished Cherry	94,258	86,301
11	5	1	Satin and Polished White	92,955	85,122
11	5	1	Satin and Polished Bubinga/Yew/Rosewood/Macassar	96,430	88,267
11	5	1	Saxony Polished Pyramid Mahogany	111,199	101,633
11	5	1	Polished Burl Walnut/Camphor	111,199	101,633
11	5	1	President Polished Ebony	98,462	90,106
11	5	1	President Polished Mahogany/Walnut	105,412	96,395
11	5	1	President Polished Bubinga	108,018	98,754
11	5	1	President Burl Walnut	122,787	112,119
11	5	1	Wilhelm II Satin and Polished Ebony	101,642	92,984
11	5	1	Wilhelm II Polished Mahogany/Walnut	109,774	100,343
11	5	1	Wilhelm II Polished Pyramid Mahogany	129,225	117,946
11	5	1	Wilhelm II Polished Burl Walnut	129,225	117,946
11	5	1	Ambassador Santos Rosewood	125,359	114,447
11	5	1	Ambassador Walnut	121,971	111,381
11	5	1	Nicolas II Satin Walnut with Burl Inlay	124,542	113,708
11	5	1	Louis XIV Rococo Satin White with Gold	139,433	127,184
11	5	1	Jubilee Polished Ebony	104,900	95,932
11	5	1	Jubilee Polished Mahogany/Walnut	111,850	102,222
11	5	1	Julius Bluthner Edition	107,837	98,590
11	5	1	Crystal Edition Elegance	131,979	120,438
11	5	1	Crystal Edition Idyllic	154,512	140,830
PH	5	1	Paul Hennigsen Design	129,000	117,742
10	5	5	Satin and Polished Ebony	100,146	91,630
10	5	5	Satin and Polished Mahogany/Walnut	108,158	98,881
10	5	5	Satin and Polished Cherry	108,659	99,334
10	5	5	Satin and Polished White	107,156	97,974
10	5	5	Satin and Polished Bubinga/Yew/Rosewood/Macassar	111,162	101,599
10	5	5	Saxony Polished Pyramid Mahogany	126,184	115,194
10	5	5	Polished Burl Walnut/Camphor	126,184	115,194
10	5	5	President Polished Ebony	111,735	102,118
10	5	5	President Polished Mahogany/Walnut	119,746	109,367
10	5	5	President Polished Bubinga	122,751	112,087
10	5	5	President Burl Walnut	137,773	125,681
10	5	5	Senator Walnut w/Leather	115,884	105,872
10	5	5	Senator Jacaranda Satin Rosewood w/Leather	125,541	114,612
10	5	5	Wilhelm II Satin and Polished Ebony	117,171	107,037
10	5	5	Wilhelm II Polished Mahogany/Walnut	126,545	115,520
10	5	5	Wilhelm II Polished Pyramid Mahogany	144,211	131,508
10	5	5	Wilhelm II Polished Burl Walnut	144,211	131,508
10	5	5	Ambassador Santos Rosewood	144,511	131,779
10	5	5	Ambassador Walnut	140,605	128,244

Model	Feet	Inches	Description	MSRP	SMP
BLÜTHNER *(continued)*					
10	5	5	Nicolas II Satin Walnut with Burl Inlay	138,803	126,614
10	5	5	Louis XIV Rococo Satin White with Gold	160,735	146,462
10	5	5	Jubilee Polished Ebony	118,173	107,944
10	5	5	Jubilee Polished Mahogany/Walnut	126,184	115,194
10	5	5	Dynasty	144,211	131,508
10	5	5	Julius Bluthner Edition	119,103	108,786
10	5	5	Crystal Edition Elegance	144,855	132,090
10	5	5	Crystal Edition Idyllic	167,388	152,482
PH	5	9	Paul Hennigsen Design	169,000	153,941
6	6	3	Satin and Polished Ebony	113,868	104,048
6	6	3	Satin and Polished Mahogany/Walnut	122,977	112,291
6	6	3	Satin and Polished Cherry	123,546	112,806
6	6	3	Satin and Polished White	121,838	111,261
6	6	3	Satin and Polished Bubinga/Yew/Rosewood/Macassar	126,393	115,383
6	6	3	Saxony Polished Pyramid Mahogany	143,473	130,840
6	6	3	Polished Burl Walnut/Camphor	143,473	130,840
6	6	3	President Polished Ebony	125,456	114,535
6	6	3	President Polished Mahogany/Walnut	134,565	122,778
6	6	3	President Polished Bubinga	137,981	125,870
6	6	3	President Burl Walnut	155,062	141,328
6	6	3	Senator Walnut w/Leather	128,760	117,525
6	6	3	Senator Jacaranda Satin Rosewood w/Leather	138,417	126,264
6	6	3	Wilhelm II Satin and Polished Ebony	133,225	121,566
6	6	3	Wilhelm II Polished Mahogany/Walnut	143,883	131,211
6	6	3	Wilhelm II Polished Pyramid Mahogany	161,500	147,154
6	6	3	Wilhelm II Polished Burl Walnut	161,500	147,154
6	6	3	Ambassador Santos Rosewood	156,727	142,834
6	6	3	Ambassador Walnut	153,721	140,114
6	6	3	Nicolas II Satin Walnut with Burl Inlay	157,821	143,824
6	6	3	Louis XIV Rococo Satin White with Gold	182,758	166,392
6	6	3	Jubilee Polished Ebony	131,894	120,361
6	6	3	Jubilee Polished Mahogany/Walnut	141,003	128,605
6	6	3	Dynasty	161,500	147,154
6	6	3	Julius Bluthner Edition	125,874	114,913
6	6	3	Crystal Edition Elegance	159,840	145,652
6	6	3	Crystal Edition Idyllic	199,800	181,814
6	6	3	Jubilee Plate, add	5,794	5,243
4	6	10	Satin and Polished Ebony	133,962	122,233
4	6	10	Satin and Polished Mahogany/Walnut	144,679	131,931
4	6	10	Satin and Polished Cherry	145,349	132,538
4	6	10	Satin and Polished White	143,339	130,719
4	6	10	Satin and Polished Bubinga/Yew/Rosewood/Macassar	148,698	135,568
4	6	10	Saxony Polished Pyramid Mahogany	168,792	153,753
4	6	10	Polished Burl Walnut/Camphor	168,792	153,753
4	6	10	President Polished Ebony	145,550	132,719

Model	Feet	Inches	Description	MSRP	SMP
BLÜTHNER *(continued)*					
4	6	10	President Polished Mahogany/Walnut	156,267	142,418
4	6	10	President Polished Bubinga	160,286	146,055
4	6	10	President Burl Walnut	180,380	164,240
4	6	10	Senator Walnut w/Leather	148,074	135,004
4	6	10	Senator Jacaranda Satin Rosewood w/Leather	157,731	143,743
4	6	10	Wilhelm II Satin and Polished Ebony	156,735	142,842
4	6	10	Wilhelm II Polished Mahogany/Walnut	169,274	154,189
4	6	10	Wilhelm II Polished Pyramid Mahogany	186,818	170,066
4	6	10	Wilhelm II Polished Burl Walnut	186,818	170,066
4	6	10	Ambassador Santos Rosewood	181,411	165,173
4	6	10	Ambassador Walnut	176,508	160,736
4	6	10	Nicolas II Satin Walnut with Burl Inlay	185,671	169,028
4	6	10	Louis XIV Rococo Satin White with Gold	215,009	195,578
4	6	10	Jubilee Polished Ebony	151,988	138,546
4	6	10	Jubilee Polished Mahogany/Walnut	162,705	148,244
4	6	10	Dynasty	186,818	170,066
4	6	10	Julius Bluthner Edition	152,903	139,374
4	6	10	Queen Victoria JB Edition Polished Rosewood	183,000	166,611
4	6	10	Crystal Edition Elegance	177,045	161,222
4	6	10	Crystal Edition Idyllic	218,892	199,092
2	7	8	Satin and Polished Ebony	150,707	137,386
2	7	8	Satin and Polished Mahogany/Walnut	162,764	148,298
2	7	8	Satin and Polished Cherry	163,517	148,979
2	7	8	Satin and Polished White	161,257	146,934
2	7	8	Satin and Polished Bubinga/Yew/Rosewood/Macassar	167,285	152,389
2	7	8	Saxony Polished Pyramid Mahogany	191,398	174,211
2	7	8	Polished Burl Walnut/Camphor	191,398	174,211
2	7	8	President Polished Ebony	162,296	147,874
2	7	8	President Polished Mahogany/Walnut	174,352	158,785
2	7	8	President Polished Bubinga	178,873	162,876
2	7	8	President Burl Walnut	202,986	184,698
2	7	8	Senator Walnut w/Leather	160,950	146,656
2	7	8	Senator Jacaranda Satin Rosewood w/Leather	170,607	155,395
2	7	8	Wilhelm II Satin and Polished Ebony	176,327	160,572
2	7	8	Wilhelm II Polished Mahogany/Walnut	190,434	173,338
2	7	8	Wilhelm II Polished Pyramid Mahogany	209,424	190,524
2	7	8	Wilhelm II Polished Burl Walnut	209,424	190,524
2	7	8	Ambassador Santos Rosewood	204,088	185,695
2	7	8	Ambassador Walnut	198,572	180,703
2	7	8	Nicolas II Satin Walnut with Burl Inlay	210,538	191,532
2	7	8	Louis XIV Rococo Satin White with Gold	241,885	219,900
2	7	8	Jubilee Polished Ebony	168,734	153,700
2	7	8	Jubilee Polished Mahogany/Walnut	180,790	164,611

Model	Feet	Inches	Description	MSRP	SMP
BLÜTHNER *(continued)*					
2	7	8	Dynasty	209,424	190,524
2	7	8	Julius Bluthner Edition	177,045	161,222
2	7	8	Queen Victoria JB Edition Polished Rosewood	202,456	184,218
2	7	8	Crystal Edition Elegance	231,768	210,745
2	7	8	Crystal Edition Idyllic	273,615	248,615
1	9	2	Satin and Polished Ebony	203,253	184,939
1	9	2	Satin and Polished Mahogany/Walnut	219,513	199,654
1	9	2	Satin and Polished Cherry	220,529	200,574
1	9	2	Satin and Polished White	217,480	197,814
1	9	2	Satin and Polished Bubinga/Yew/Rosewood/Macassar	225,610	205,172
1	9	2	Saxony Polished Pyramid Mahogany	258,131	234,603
1	9	2	Polished Burl Walnut/Camphor	264,228	240,120
1	9	2	President Polished Ebony	216,040	196,511
1	9	2	President Polished Mahogany/Walnut	232,300	211,226
1	9	2	President Polished Bubinga	238,398	216,745
1	9	2	President Burl Walnut	277,016	251,693
1	9	2	Wilhelm II Satin and Polished Ebony	237,805	216,208
1	9	2	Wilhelm II Polished Mahogany/Walnut	256,830	233,425
1	9	2	Wilhelm II Polished Pyramid Mahogany	278,022	252,604
1	9	2	Wilhelm II Polished Burl Walnut	284,120	258,122
1	9	2	Ambassador Santos Rosewood	279,757	254,174
1	9	2	Ambassador Walnut	274,391	249,318
1	9	2	Nicolas II Satin Walnut with Burl Inlay	290,651	264,033
1	9	2	Jubilee Polished Ebony	223,144	202,940
1	9	2	Jubilee Polished Mahogany/Walnut	239,404	217,655
1	9	2	Dynasty	288,600	262,176
1	9	2	Julius Bluthner Edition	230,798	209,867
1	9	2	Queen Victoria JB Edition Polished Rosewood	244,938	222,663
1	9	2	Crystal Edition Elegance	273,060	248,113
1	9	2	Crystal Edition Idyllic	316,350	287,290
Grands			e-volution Hybrid Piano System, add	8,800	7,964

BÖSENDORFER

Verticals

Model		Inches	Description	MSRP	SMP
130		52	Satin and Polished Ebony	76,999	72,998
130		52	Satin and Polished White, other colors	91,999	86,998
130		52	Polished, Satin, Open-pore: Walnut, Cherry, Mahogany, Pomele	98,999	92,998
130		52	Polished , Satin, Open-pore: Pyramid Mahogany, Burl Walnut, Birdseye Maple, Macassar, Madronna, Vavona, Wenge	103,999	98,998

BÖSENDORFER (continued)

Grands

Model	Feet	Inches	Description	MSRP	SMP
155	5	1	Satin and Polished Ebony	121,999	114,998
155	5	1	Satin and Polished White, other colors	136,999	128,998
155	5	1	Polished, Satin, Open-pore: Walnut, Cherry, Mahogany, Pomele	146,999	138,998
155	5	1	Polished , Satin, Open-pore: Pyramid Mahogany, Burl Walnut, Birdseye Maple, Macassar, Madronna, Vavona, Wenge	159,999	150,998
155	5	1	Chrome: Satin and Polished Ebony	138,999	130,998
170	5	7	Satin and Polished Ebony	126,999	120,998
170	5	7	Satin and Polished White, other colors	142,999	134,998
170	5	7	Polished, Satin, Open-pore: Walnut, Cherry, Mahogany, Pomele	153,999	144,998
170	5	7	Polished , Satin, Open-pore: Bubinga, Pyramid Mahogany, Santos Rosewood, Burl Walnut, Birdseye Maple, Macassar, Madronna, Vavona, Wenge	164,999	154,998
170	5	7	Chrome: Satin and Polished Ebony	142,999	134,998
170	5	7	Johann Strauss: Satin and Polished Ebony w/Maple	152,999	144,998
170	5	7	Johann Strauss: Any finish and veneer	178,999	168,998
170	5	7	Liszt: Polished Vavona	182,999	172,998
170	5	7	Chopin, Louis XVI: Satin Pommele	207,999	196,998
170	5	7	Baroque: Light Satin Ivory; Vienna: Polished Amboyna	232,999	218,998
170	5	7	Artisan Satin and Polished	297,999	280,998
185CS	6	1	Conservatory Satin Ebony	116,999	110,998
185	6	1	Satin and Polished Ebony	133,999	126,998
185	6	1	Satin and Polished White, other colors	149,999	140,998
185	6	1	Polished, Satin, Open-pore: Walnut, Cherry, Mahogany, Pomele	157,999	148,998
185	6	1	Polished , Satin, Open-pore: Pyramid Mahogany, Burl Walnut, Birdseye Maple, Macassar, Madronna, Vavona, Wenge	169,999	160,998
185	6	1	Chrome: Satin and Polished Ebony	149,999	140,998
185	6	1	Johann Strauss: Satin and Polished Ebony w/Maple	159,999	150,998
185	6	1	Johann Strauss: Any finish and veneer	185,000	174,998
185	6	1	Liszt: Polished Vavona	189,999	178,998
185	6	1	Edge: Satin and Polished Ebony	212,999	200,998
185	6	1	Chopin, Louis XVI: Satin Pommele	215,999	202,998
185	6	1	Baroque: Satin Light Ivory; Vienna: Polished Amboyna	236,999	222,998
185	6	1	Porsche Design: Diamond Black Metallic Gloss	248,999	234,998
185	6	1	Artisan Satin and Polished	306,999	288,998
200CS	6	7	Conservatory Satin Ebony	122,999	116,998
200	6	7	Satin and Polished Ebony	144,999	136,998
200	6	7	Satin and Polished White, other colors	161,999	152,998
200	6	7	Polished, Satin, Open-pore: Walnut, Cherry, Mahogany, Pomele	172,999	162,998
200	6	7	Polished , Satin, Open-pore: Pyramid Mahogany, Burl Walnut, Birdseye Maple, Macassar, Madronna, Vavona, Wenge	185,999	174,998

Model	Feet	Inches	Description	MSRP	SMP
BÖSENDORFER *(continued)*					
200	6	7	Chrome Satin and Polished Ebony	145,596	120,744
200	6	7	Chrome: Satin and Polished Ebony	159,999	150,998
200	6	7	Johann Strauss: Satin and Polished Ebony w/Maple	170,999	160,998
200	6	7	Johann Strauss: Any finish and veneer	201,999	190,998
200	6	7	Dragonfly: Maple and Polished Ebony	206,999	194,998
200	6	7	Liszt: Polished Vavona	206,999	194,998
200	6	7	Beethoven Polished Ebony, Klimt "Woman in Gold"	176,999	166,998
200	6	7	Beethoven: Chrome; Cocteau: White	204,999	192,998
200	6	7	Edge: Satin and Polished Ebony	233,999	220,998
200	6	7	Chopin, Louis XVI: Satin Pommele	236,999	222,998
200	6	7	Baroque: Satin Light Ivory; Vienna: Polished Amboyna	259,999	244,998
200	6	7	Artisan Satin and Polished	325,999	306,998
214VC CS	7		Conservatory Satin Ebony	132,999	126,998
214VC	7		Satin and Polished Ebony	158,999	150,998
214VC	7		Satin and Polished White, other colors	181,999	170,998
214VC	7		Polished, Satin, Open-pore: Walnut, Cherry, Mahogany, Pomele	193,999	182,998
214VC	7		Polished , Satin, Open-pore: Pyramid Mahogany, Burl Walnut, Birdseye Maple, Macassar, Madronna, Vavona, Wenge	211,999	198,998
214VC	7		Chrome: Satin and Polished Ebony	180,999	170,998
214VC	7		Johann Strauss: Satin and Polished Ebony w/Maple	189,999	178,998
214VC	7		Johann Strauss: Any finish and veneer	227,999	214,998
214VC	7		Liszt: Polished Vavona	233,999	220,998
214VC	7		Beethoven: Polished Ebony, Klimt "Woman in Gold"	191,999	182,998
214VC	7		Beethoven: Chrome; Cocteau: White	225,999	212,998
214VC	7		Edge: Satin and Polished Ebony	258,999	246,998
214VC	7		Chopin, Louis XVI: Satin Pommele	266,999	250,998
214VC	7		Baroque: Satin Light Ivory; Vienna: Polished Amboyna	292,999	274,998
214VC	7		Porsche Design: Diamond Black Metallic Gloss	308,999	290,998
214VC	7		Audi Design Polished Ebony	372,999	352,998
214VC	7		Artisan Satin and Polished	372,999	352,998
225	7	4	Satin and Polished Ebony	178,999	168,998
225	7	4	Satin and Polished White, other colors	197,999	186,998
225	7	4	Polished, Satin, Open-pore: Walnut, Cherry, Mahogany, Pomele	212,999	200,998
225	7	4	Polished , Satin, Open-pore: Pyramid Mahogany, Burl Walnut, Birdseye Maple, Macassar, Madronna, Vavona, Wenge	229,999	216,998
225	7	4	Chrome: Satin and Polished Ebony	193,999	182,999
225	7	4	Johann Strauss: Satin and Polished Ebony w/Maple	204,999	192,998
225	7	4	Johann Strauss: Any finish and veneer	248,999	234,998
225	7	4	Liszt: Polished Vavona	255,999	240,998
225	7	4	Chopin, Louis XVI: Satin Pommele	291,999	274,998
225	7	4	Baroque: Satin Light Ivory; Vienna: Polished Amboyna	319,999	300,998
225	7	4	Artisan Satin and Polished	398,999	374,998
225	7	4	Grand Bohemian: Polished Ebony	420,000	420,000

Model	Feet	Inches	Description	MSRP	SMP
BÖSENDORFER *(continued)*					
280VC	9	2	Satin and Polished Ebony	229,999	216,998
280VC	9	2	Satin and Polished White, other colors	254,999	240,998
280VC	9	2	Polished, Satin, Open-pore: Walnut, Cherry, Mahogany, Pomele	274,999	258,998
280VC	9	2	Polished , Satin, Open-pore: Pyramid Mahogany, Burl Walnut, Birdseye Maple, Macassar, Madronna, Vavona, Wenge	297,999	280,998
280VC	9	2	Johann Strauss: Satin and Polished Ebony w/Maple	270,999	254,998
280VC	9	2	Johann Strauss: Any finish and veneer	323,999	304,998
280VC	9	2	Liszt: Polished Vavona	331,999	312,998
280VC	9	2	Chopin, Louis XVI: Satin Pommele	379,999	356,998
280VC	9	2	Baroque: Satin Light Ivory; Vienna: Polished Amboyna	412,999	390,998
280VC	9	2	Porsche Design: Diamond Black Metallic Gloss	437,999	412,998
280VC	9	2	Artisan Satin and Polished	472,999	444,998
290	9	6	Satin and Polished Ebony	262,999	246,998
290	9	6	Satin and Polished White, other colors	288,999	272,998
290	9	6	Polished, Satin, Open-pore: Walnut, Cherry, Mahogany, Pomele	312,999	294,998
290	9	6	Polished , Satin, Open-pore: Pyramid Mahogany, Burl Walnut, Birdseye Maple, Macassar, Madronna, Vavona, Wenge	338,999	318,998
290	9	6	Johann Strauss: Satin and Polished Ebony w/Maple	302,999	284,998
290	9	6	Johann Strauss: Any finish and veneer	369,999	346,998
290	9	6	Liszt: Polished Vavona	377,999	354,998
290	9	6	Chopin, Louis XVI: Satin Pommele	429,999	404,998
290	9	6	Baroque: Satin Light Ivory; Vienna: Polished Amboyna	472,999	444,998
290	9	6	Artisan Satin and Polished	536,999	506,998
Select models			Disklavier Enspire PRO, add	39,999	37,998

BOSTON

Boston MSRP is the price at the New York retail store.

Verticals

Model	Feet	Inches	Description	MSRP	SMP
UP-118E PE		46	Satin and Polished Ebony	11,950	11,950
UP-118E PE		46	Polished Mahogany	13,800	13,800
UP-118E PE		46	Satin and Polished Walnut	13,800	13,800
UP-118S PE		46	Satin Black Oak	7,850	7,850
UP-118S PE		46	Satin Mahogany	9,400	9,400
UP-126E PE		50	Polished Ebony	14,300	14,300
UP-126E PE		50	Polished Mahogany	16,600	16,600
UP-132E PE		52	Polished Ebony	15,900	15,900

Grands

Model	Feet	Inches	Description	MSRP	SMP
GP-156 PE	5	1	Satin and Polished Ebony	21,800	21,800
GP-163 PE	5	4	Satin and Polished Ebony	26,600	26,600
GP-163 PE	5	4	Satin and Polished Mahogany	29,100	29,100
GP-163 PE	5	4	Satin and Polished Walnut	29,500	29,500

Model	Feet	Inches	Description	MSRP	SMP

BOSTON (continued)

Model	Feet	Inches	Description	MSRP	SMP
GP-163 PE	5	4	Polished White	32,800	32,800
GP-178 PE	5	10	Satin and Polished Ebony	31,100	31,100
GP-178 PE	5	10	Satin and Polished Mahogany	33,600	33,600
GP-178 PE	5	10	Satin and Polished Walnut	34,100	34,100
GP-193 PE	6	4	Satin and Polished Ebony	40,500	40,500
GP-215 PE	7	1	Polished Ebony	52,950	52,950

BRODMANN

Verticals

Model	Feet	Inches	Description	MSRP	SMP
CE 118		47	Polished Ebony	8,990	5,900
PE 118V		47	Vienna Polished Ebony	12,490	7,780
PE 121		48	Polished Ebony	11,490	7,100
PE 121		48	Polished Mahogany/Walnut	12,490	7,700
PE 121		48	Polished White	12,990	7,900
PE 121		48	Polished Two Tone (Apple Tree Saphire/Ebony)	13,490	8,300
PE 124V		48	Vienna Polished Ebony	14,490	8,780
PE 124V		48	ViennaPolished Bubinga	15,490	9,380
PE 125		49	Polished Ebony	12,490	7,700
PE 126I		49	Polished Ebony w/Institutional Wide Music Desk	13,990	8,500
PE 130		52	Polished Ebony	17,490	10,500
PE 132V		52	Vienna Polished Ebony	18,990	11,380
AS 132		52	Polished Ebony	29,490	16,980

Grands

Model	Feet	Inches	Description	MSRP	SMP
CE 148	4	10	Polished Ebony	22,490	15,993
CE 175	5	9	Polished Ebony	26,490	18,660
PE 150	5		Polished Ebony	26,990	18,993
PE 162	5	4	Polished Ebony	31,490	21,993
PE 162	5	4	Polished Mahogany/Walnut	34,990	24,327
PE 162	5	4	Polished White	33,990	23,660
PE 162	5	4	Polished Bubinga	35,490	24,660
PE 162	5	4	Polished Two Tone (Ebony/Bubinga)	32,490	22,660
PE 187	6	2	Polished Ebony	35,990	24,993
PE 187 IV	6	2	Polished Ebony w/Carbon-Fiber Action	42,990	29,660
PE 187	6	2	Polished Mahogany/Walnut	39,490	27,327
PE 187	6	2	Polished White	38,490	26,660
PE 187	6	2	Polished Bubinga	40,490	27,993
PE 187	6	2	Strauss Polished Ebony	38,490	26,660
PE 187	6	2	Strauss Polished Two Tone (Ebony/Bubinga)	39,990	27,660
PE 212	7		Polished Ebony	56,990	38,993
PE 228	7	5	Polished Ebony	72,990	49,660
AS 188	6	2	Polished Ebony	66,990	45,660
AS 211	7		Polished Ebony	84,990	57,660
AS 227	7	6	Polished Ebony	96,990	65,660

Model	Feet	Inches	Description	MSRP	SMP

BRODMANN *(continued)*

Model	Feet	Inches	Description	MSRP	SMP
AS 275	9		Polished Ebony	159,990	86,980
Grands			With Carbon-Fiber Action, add	7,000	3,580

CLINE
Verticals

Model	Feet	Inches	Description	MSRP	SMP
CL118		46.5	Polished Ebony		6,300
CL118		46.5	Polished Ebony w/Nickel		6,500
CL118		46.5	Polished Walnut/Mahogany		6,500
CL121/123		48	Polished Ebony		7,390
CL121/123		48	Polished Ebony w/Nickel		7,590
CL121/123		48	Polished Mahogany/Walnut		7,590
CL121/123		48	Polished Mahogany/Walnut w/Detail Trim		7,590

Grands

Model	Feet	Inches	Description	MSRP	SMP
CL 150	4	11	Polished Ebony		12,300
CL 150	4	11	Polished Mahogany/Walnut		12,500

CRISTOFORI
Verticals

Model	Feet	Inches	Description	MSRP	SMP
V430R		43	French Provincial Satin Cherry	4,999	4,999
V450		45	Polished Ebony	3,999	3,999
V450		45	Polished Mahogany	4,199	4,199
V465		46.5	Polished Ebony	4,499	4,220
V465		46.5	Polished Mahogany	4,699	4,442
V480LS		48	Polished Ebony	4,999	4,530
V480LS		48	Polished Mahogany	5,199	4,668

Grands

Model	Feet	Inches	Description	MSRP	SMP
G410L	4	10	Polished Ebony	8,990	8,750
G410L	4	10	Polished Mahogany	9,490	9,418
G53L	5	3	Satin and Polished Ebony	9,990	9,990
G53L	5	3	Polished Mahogany/Snow White	10,490	10,490
G57L	5	7	Satin and Polished Ebony	11,990	10,642
G57L	5	7	Polished Mahogany	12,490	11,406
G62L	6	2	Satin and Polished Ebony	13,990	11,902

CUNNINGHAM
Verticals

Model	Feet	Inches	Description	MSRP	SMP
Liberty Console		44	Satin Ebony	6,590	6,590
Liberty Console		44	Polished Ebony	5,890	5,890
Liberty Console		44	Satin Mahogany	6,890	6,890
Liberty Console		44	Polished Mahogany	6,190	6,190

Model	Feet	Inches	Description	MSRP	SMP
CUNNINGHAM *(continued)*					
Studio Upright		50	Satin Ebony	10,690	10,690
Studio Upright		50	Polished Ebony	9,890	9,890
Studio Upright		50	Satin Mahogany	10,990	10,990
Studio Upright		50	Polished Mahogany	10,190	10,190
Grands					
Baby Grand	5		Satin Ebony	20,390	20,390
Baby Grand	5		Polished Ebony	19,190	19,190
Baby Grand	5		Satin Mahogany	21,090	21,090
Baby Grand	5		Polished Mahogany	19,890	19,890
Studio Grand	5	4	Satin Ebony	22,090	22,090
Studio Grand	5	4	Polished Ebony	20,890	20,890
Studio Grand	5	4	Satin Mahogany	22,790	22,790
Studio Grand	5	4	Polished Mahogany	21,590	21,590
Parlour Grand	5	10	Satin Ebony	26,390	26,390
Parlour Grand	5	10	Polished Ebony	25,190	25,190
Parlour Grand	5	10	Satin Mahogany	27,090	27,090
Parlour Grand	5	10	Polished Mahogany	25,890	25,890
Chamber Grand	7		Satin Ebony	41,290	41,290
Chamber Grand	7		Polished Ebony	39,790	39,790
Concert Grand	9		Satin Ebony	62,990	62,990
Concert Grand	9		Polished Ebony	60,990	60,990

DISKLAVIER — see Yamaha; see also Bösendorfer

ESSEX

Essex MSRP is the price at the New York retail store.

Verticals

Model	Feet	Inches	Description	MSRP	SMP
EUP-108C		42	Continental Polished Ebony	5,690	5,690
EUP-111E		44	Polished Ebony	6,390	6,390
EUP-111E		44	Polished Sapele Mahogany	6,790	6,540
EUP-116E		45	Polished Ebony	7,190	6,760
EUP-116E		45	Polished Sapele Mahogany	7,490	6,860
EUP-116E		45	Polished White	7,790	7,100
EUP-116CT		45	Contemporary Satin Lustre Sapele Mahogany	8,250	7,600
EUP-116QA		45	Queen Anne Satin Lustre Cherry	7,950	7,740
EUP-116EC		45	English Country Satin Lustre Walnut	7,950	7,560
EUP-116FF		45	Formal French Satin Lustre Brown Cherry	8,250	7,780
EUP-123E		48	Satin Ebony w/Chrome Hardware	8,650	7,980
EUP-123E		48	Polished Ebony	7,690	7,300
EUP-123E		48	Polished Ebony w/Chrome Hardware	7,790	7,400
EUP-123E		48	Polished Sapele Mahogany	8,750	7,800
EUP-123FL		48	Empire Satin Walnut	8,850	7,860

Model	Feet	Inches	Description	MSRP	SMP
ESSEX (*continued*)					
EUP-123FL		48	Empire Satin Sapele Mahogany	8,850	8,080
EUP-123S		48	Institutional Studio Polished Ebony	7,690	7,620
Grands					
EGP-155	5	1	Satin and Polished Ebony	13,900	13,900
EGP-155	5	1	Polished Sapele Mahogany	15,250	15,250
EGP-155	5	1	Satin Lustre Sapele Mahogany	15,600	15,600
EGP-155	5	1	Polished White	18,600	16,480
EGP-155F	5	1	French Provincial Satin Lustre Brown Cherry	17,700	17,620
EGP-173	5	8	Satin Lustre and Polished Ebony	17,620	17,620

ESTONIA

The Estonia factory can make custom-designed finishes with exotic veneers; prices upon request.
Prices here include Jansen adjustable artist benches.

Grands

Model	Feet	Inches	Description	MSRP	SMP
L168	5	6	Satin and Polished Ebony	43,800	41,538
L168	5	6	Satin and Polished Mahogany/Walnut	47,380	44,641
L168	5	6	Polished Kewazinga Bubinga	51,395	48,564
L168	5	6	Polished Pyramid Mahogany	56,873	53,814
L168	5	6	Satin and Polished White	49,880	46,927
L168	5	6	Hidden Beauty Polished Ebony w/Bubinga	48,473	45,603
L190	6	3	Satin and Polished Ebony	53,789	50,496
L190	6	3	Satin and Polished Mahogany/Walnut	57,298	54,212
L190	6	3	Polished Pyramid Mahogany	68,400	63,318
L190	6	3	Polished Santos Rosewood	68,400	63,146
L190	6	3	Polished Kewazinga Bubinga	61,688	58,256
L190	6	3	Hidden Beauty Polished Ebony w/Bubinga	56,570	53,399
L210	6	10	Satin and Polished Ebony	63,300	60,796
L210	6	10	Satin and Polished Mahogany/Walnut/White	69,630	66,778
L210	6	10	Polished Pyramid Mahogany	79,125	75,746
L210	6	10	Polished Kewazinga Bubinga	74,700	71,560
L210	6	10	Hidden Beauty Polished Ebony w/Bubinga	67,230	64,293
L225	7	4	Satin and Polished Ebony	79,689	74,297
L225	7	4	Satin and Polished Mahogany/Walnut/White	85,727	80,667
L225	7	4	Polished Pyramid Mahogany	95,156	90,710
L225	7	4	Polished Kewazinga Bubinga	86,100	83,597
L225	7	4	Hidden Beauty Polished Ebony w/Bubinga	84,635	79,451
L274	9		Satin and Polished Ebony	127,140	112,678
L274	9		Satin and Polished Mahogany/Walnut	139,430	124,475
L274	9		Polished Pyramid Mahogany	144,254	137,514
L274	9		Satin and Polished White	131,177	119,193

Model	Feet	Inches	Description	MSRP	SMP

FANDRICH & SONS

These are the prices on the Fandrich & Sons website. Other finishes available at additional cost. See website for details.

Verticals

Model	Feet	Inches	Description	MSRP	SMP
118-S		46	Polished Ebony with Nickel Trim	5,640	5,640
122		48	Polished Ebony	6,640	6,640
122		48	Polished Mahogany/Walnut/Cherry	6,840	6,840
131-V		52	Polished Ebony	12,890	12,890

Grands

Model	Feet	Inches	Description	MSRP	SMP
170-S	5	7	Polished Ebony	18,890	18,890
188-S	6	2	Polished Ebony	22,490	22,490
212-S	7		Polished Ebony	34,990	34,990
212-E	7		Polished Ebony	36,490	36,490

FAZIOLI

Fazioli is willing to make custom-designed cases with exotic veneers, marquetry, and other embellishments. Prices on request to Fazioli.

Grands

Model	Feet	Inches	Description	MSRP	SMP
F156	5	2	Satin and Polished Ebony	120,000	113,951
F156	5	2	Satin and Polished White/Red	138,000	130,609
F156	5	2	Satin and Polished Walnut/Cherry/Mahogany	150,000	141,414
F156	5	2	Satin and Polished Pyramid Mahogany/Macassar	168,000	157,846
F156	5	2	Satin and Polished Briers: Mahogany/California Walnut/Sequoia	180,000	168,651
F156	5	2	Satin and Polished Olive	191,400	179,916
F183	6		Satin and Polished Ebony	124,200	116,602
F183	6		Satin and Polished White/Red	141,300	133,260
F183	6		Satin and Polished Walnut/Cherry/Mahogany	153,600	144,515
F183	6		Satin and Polished Pyramid Mahogany/Macassar	172,100	161,173
F183	6		Satin and Polished Briers: Mahogany/California Walnut/Sequoia	184,300	172,428
F183	6		Satin and Polished Olive	195,200	183,488
F212	7		Satin and Polished Ebony	140,100	130,458
F212	7		Satin and Polished White/Red	151,000	142,839
F212	7		Satin and Polished Walnut/Cherry/Mahogany	164,800	155,220
F212	7		Satin and Polished Pyramid Mahogany/Macassar	178,500	167,600
F212	7		Satin and Polished Briers: Mahogany/California Walnut/Sequoia	192,200	179,981
F212	7		Satin and Polished Olive	203,700	191,478
F228	7	6	Satin and Polished Ebony	156,700	146,415
F228	7	6	Satin and Polished White/Red	169,000	160,372
F228	7	6	Satin and Polished Walnut/Cherry/Mahogany	184,300	174,553
F228	7	6	Satin and Polished Pyramid Mahogany/Macassar	199,700	188,510
F228	7	6	Satin and Polished Briers: Mahogany/California Walnut/Sequoia	215,000	202,466
F228	7	6	Satin and Polished Olive	230,500	249,213

Model	Feet	Inches	Description	MSRP	SMP
FAZIOLI *(continued)*					
F278	9	2	Satin and Polished Ebony	211,600	193,162
F278	9	2	Satin and Polished White/Red	225,900	211,846
F278	9	2	Satin and Polished Walnut/Cherry/Mahogany	246,500	230,529
F278	9	2	Satin and Polished Pyramid Mahogany/Macassar	267,000	249,213
F278	9	2	Satin and Polished Briers: Mahogany/California Walnut/Sequoia	287,600	267,897
F278	9	2	Satin and Polished Olive	306,500	285,045
F308	10	2	Satin and Polished Ebony	231,400	207,418
F308	10	2	Satin and Polished White/Red	247,100	227,677
F308	10	2	Satin and Polished Walnut/Cherry/Mahogany	269,500	247,712
F308	10	2	Satin and Polished Pyramid Mahogany/Macassar	292,000	267,521
F308	10	2	Satin and Polished Briers: Mahogany/California Walnut/Sequoia	314,400	287,330
F308	10	2	Satin and Polished Olive	326,800	297,388

FEURICH

Verticals

Model	Feet	Inches	Description	MSRP	SMP
115 Premiere		45	Polished Ebony	8,800	6,172
122 Universal		48	Polished Ebony	9,800	7,055
123 Vienna		48.5	Polished Ebony	15,500	15,128
133 Concert		52	Polished Ebony	12,500	9,956

Grands

Model	Feet	Inches	Description	MSRP	SMP
162 Dynamic I	5	4	Polished Ebony	19,500	15,380
179 Dynamic II	5	10	Polished Ebony	23,500	18,407
218 Concert I	7	2	Polished Ebony	37,900	31,021
Grands			Harmonic Pedal, add	3,000	1,892

FÖRSTER, AUGUST

Prices do not include bench. Euro = $1.14

Verticals

Model	Feet	Inches	Description	MSRP	SMP
116 C		46	Chippendale Satin Ebony	31,543	
116 C		46	Chippendale Satin Walnut	33,535	
116 D		46	Continental Satin Ebony	21,815	
116 D		46	Continental Polished Ebony	24,149	
116 D		46	Continental Satin Mahogany/Walnut/Oak/Cherry	23,949	
116 D		46	Continental Polished Mahogany/Walnut	26,456	
116 D		46	Continental Satin Beech	22,235	
116 D		46	Continental Polished White with bench	26,220	
116 E		46	Satin Ebony	26,036	
116 E		46	Polished Ebony	28,265	
116 E		46	Satin Mahogany/Walnut/Oak/Cherry	28,085	
116 E		46	Polished Mahogany/Walnut	30,546	

Model	Feet	Inches	Description	MSRP	SMP

FÖRSTER, AUGUST *(continued)*

Model	Feet	Inches	Description	MSRP	SMP
116 E		46	Satin Beech		26,456
116 E		46	Polished White with bench		30,337
125 F		49	Polished Ebony		32,618
125 G		49	Satin Ebony		29,681
125 G		49	Polished Ebony		31,936
125 G		49	Satin Mahogany/Walnut/Oak/Cherry		32,306
125 G		49	Polished Mahogany/Walnut		34,951
125 G		49	Satin Beech		30,101
125 G		49	Polished White with bench		34,427
125 G		49	With Oval Medallion, add		1,600
134 K		53	Polished Ebony		49,661

Grands

Model	Feet	Inches	Description	MSRP	SMP
170	5	8	Satin Ebony		62,194
170	5	8	Polished Ebony		66,573
170	5	8	Satin Mahogany/Walnut/Cherry		66,415
170	5	8	Polished Mahogany/Walnut		70,584
170	5	8	Polished White with bench		72,000
170	5	8	Classik Polished Ebony		76,510
170	5	8	Classik Polished Mahogany/Walnut		87,994
170	5	8	Classik Polished White with bench		81,885
190	6	4	Satin Ebony		70,689
190	6	4	Polished Ebony		75,147
190	6	4	Satin Mahogany/Walnut/Cherry		74,779
190	6	4	Polished Mahogany/Walnut		79,001
190	6	4	Polished White with bench		80,495
190	6	4	Classik Polished Ebony		84,874
190	6	4	Classik Polished Mahogany/Walnut		99,557
190	6	4	Classik Polished White with bench		90,328
190	6	4	Rokoko Polished White with bench		231,056
215	7	2	Polished Ebony		90,223
215	7	2	Polished White with bench		100,632
275	9	1	Polished Ebony		163,272

GEYER, A.

Verticals

Model	Feet	Inches	Description	MSRP	SMP
GU 115		45	Polished Ebony	6,185	4,990
GU 115		45	Polished Mahogany/Walnut	6,685	5,290
GU 115		45	Polished White	6,485	5,190
GU 123		47	Polished Ebony	6,785	5,390
GU 123		47	Polished Mahogany/Walnut	7,235	5,690
GU 123		47	Polished White	7,085	5,590
GU 133		52	Polished Ebony	7,685	5,990
GU 133		52	Polished Mahogany/Walnut	8,285	6,390
GU 133		52	Polished White	7,985	6,190

Model	Feet	Inches	Description	MSRP	SMP

GEYER, A. *(continued)*
Grands

Model	Feet	Inches	Description	MSRP	SMP
GG 150	4	11	Polished Ebony	12,785	9,590
GG 150	4	11	Polished Mahogany/Walnut	13,685	9,990
GG 150	4	11	Polished White	13,235	9,870
GG 160	5	3	Polished Ebony	14,535	10,590
GG 160	5	3	Polished Mahogany/Walnut	15,285	10,990
GG 160	5	3	Polished White	15,035	10,890
GG 170	5	7	Polished Ebony	16,385	11,790
GG 170	5	7	Polished Mahogany/Walnut	16,715	12,010
GG 170	5	7	Polished White	16,835	12,090
GG 185	6	1	Polished Ebony	18,785	13,390
GG 185	6	1	Polished Mahogany/Walnut	19,585	13,990
GG 185	6	1	Polished White	19,385	13,790
GG 230	7	7	Polished Ebony	29,225	25,990

GROTRIAN
Grotrian Verticals

Model	Feet	Inches	Description	MSRP	SMP
Studio 110		43.5	Satin Ebony	16,373	15,691
Studio 110		43.5	Satin White	16,675	15,980
Friedrich Grotrian		43.5	Polished Ebony	17,119	16,406
Friedrich Grotrian		43.5	Open-pore Walnut	17,119	16,406
Cristal		44	Continental Satin Ebony	22,087	21,167
Cristal		44	Continental Polished Ebony	23,066	22,105
Cristal		44	Continental Open-pore Walnut	23,066	22,105
Cristal		44	Continental Polished Walnut/White	25,272	24,219
Contour		45	Polished Ebony	24,782	23,750
Contour		45	Open-pore Walnut	24,782	23,750
Contour		45	Polished Walnut/White	27,150	26,018
Canto		45	Satin Ebony	24,618	23,593
Canto		45	Polished Ebony	25,762	24,688
Canto		45	Open-pore Walnut	25,762	24,688
Carat		45.5	Polished Ebony	29,028	27,819
Carat		45.5	Open-pore Walnut	29,028	27,819
Carat		45.5	Polished Walnut/White	31,562	30,247
College		48	Satin Ebony	31,378	30,070
College		48	Polished Ebony	33,013	31,639
College		48	Open-pore Walnut	33,013	31,639
Classic		49	Polished Ebony	39,220	37,587
Classic		49	Open-pore Walnut	39,220	37,587
Classic		49	Polished Walnut/White	42,241	40,480
Concertino		52	Polished Ebony	49,386	47,329
Concertino		52	Open-pore Walnut	49,386	47,329
Verticals			Chippendale/Rococo/Empire, add	1,411	1,352
Verticals			Sostenuto, add	1,699	1,628

Model	Feet	Inches	Description	MSRP	SMP

GROTRIAN *(continued)*

Wilhelm Grotrian Verticals

Model	Feet	Inches	Description	MSRP	SMP
WG-18		46.5	Polished Ebony		9,998
WG-23		48.5	Polished Ebony		11,198
WG-26		49.5	Polished Ebony		12,198
WG-32		52	Polished Ebony		13,798

Wilhelm Grotrian Studio Verticals

Model	Feet	Inches	Description	MSRP	SMP
WGS-116		46	Polished Ebony		6,798
WGS-120		47	Polished Ebony		7,598
WGS-122		48	Polished Ebony		8,398

Grotrian Grands

Model	Feet	Inches	Description	MSRP	SMP
Chambre	5	5	Satin Ebony	72,544	72,544
Chambre	5	5	Polished Ebony	80,058	80,058
Chambre	5	5	Open-pore Walnut	80,058	80,058
Chambre	5	5	Polished Walnut/White	87,736	87,736
Cabinet	6	3	Satin Ebony	84,306	84,306
Cabinet	6	3	Polished Ebony	93,946	93,946
Cabinet	6	3	Studio Lacquer Ebony	65,310	65,310
Cabinet	6	3	Open-pore Walnut	93,946	93,946
Cabinet	6	3	Polished Walnut/White	102,931	102,931
Charis	6	10	Satin Ebony	99,377	99,377
Charis	6	10	Polished Ebony	108,524	108,524
Charis	6	10	Studio Lacquer Ebony	79,764	79,764
Charis	6	10	Open-pore Walnut	108,524	108,524
Concert	7	4	Satin Ebony	118,354	118,354
Concert	7	4	Polished Ebony	134,001	134,001
Concert	7	4	Open-pore Walnut	134,001	134,001
Concert Royal	9	1	Polished Ebony	179,914	179,914
Concert Royal	9	1	Open-pore Walnut	179,914	179,914
Grands			Chippendale/Empire, add	4,896	4,896
Grands			CS Style, add	5,472	5,472
Grands			Rococo, add	16,416	16,416

Wilhelm Grotrian Grands

Model	Feet	Inches	Description	MSRP	SMP
WG-170	5	7	Polished Ebony		30,800
WG-188	6	2	Polished Ebony		38,980
WG-211	6	11	Polished Ebony		56,980

Wilhelm Grotrian Studio Grands

Model	Feet	Inches	Description	MSRP	SMP
WGS-152	5		Polished Ebony		16,398
WGS-165	5	5	Polished Ebony		19,398

Model	Feet	Inches	Description	MSRP	SMP

HAESSLER

Prices do not include bench.

Verticals

Model	Inches	Description	MSRP	SMP
H 118	47	Polished Ebony	24,640	23,198
H 118	47	Satin Mahogany/Walnut	25,784	24,230
H 118	47	Polished Mahogany/Walnut	29,906	27,942
H 118	47	Satin Cherry	26,242	24,642
H 118	47	Polished Cherry	30,364	28,356
H 118	47	Satin Oak/Beech	24,456	23,032
H 118	47	Polished White	26,929	25,260
H 118	47	Polished Bubinga	30,593	28,562
H 118	47	Satin Mahogany w/Vavona Inlay	27,616	25,880
H 118	47	Polished Mahogany w/Vavona Inlay	31,280	29,180
H 118	47	Polished Burl Walnut	31,051	28,974
H 118	47	Satin Burl Walnut w/Walnut Inlay	27,616	25,880
H 118	47	Polished Burl Walnut w/Walnut Inlay	31,280	29,180
H 118	47	Satin Cherry and Yew	27,708	25,962
H 118	47	Polished Cherry and Yew	31,280	29,180
H 124	49	Polished Ebony	26,929	25,260
H 124	49	Satin Mahogany/Walnut	27,937	26,168
H 124	49	Polished Mahogany/Walnut	32,196	30,006
H 124	49	Satin Cherry	28,074	26,292
H 124	49	Polished Cherry	32,654	30,418
H 124	49	Satin Oak/Beech	27,845	26,086
H 124	49	Polished White	29,219	27,324
H 124	49	Polished Bubinga	32,883	30,624
H 124	49	Polished Pyramid Mahogany	36,410	33,802
H 124	49	Satin Mahogany w/Vavona Inlay	29,448	27,530
H 124	49	Polished Mahogany w/Vavona Inlay	34,715	32,274
H 124	49	Polished Burl Walnut	35,952	33,388
H 124	49	Satin Burl Walnut w/Walnut Inlay	29,448	27,530
H 124	49	Polished Burl Walnut w/Walnut Inlay	34,715	32,274
H 124	49	Satin Cherry and Yew	29,448	27,530
H 124	49	Polished Cherry and Yew	35,952	33,388
K 124	49	Polished Ebony	29,128	27,242
K 124	49	Satin Mahogany/Walnut	30,135	28,148
K 124	49	Polished Mahogany/Walnut	34,395	31,986
K 124	49	Satin Cherry	30,273	28,272
K 124	49	Polished Cherry	34,853	32,398
K 124	49	Satin Oak/Beech	30,044	28,066
K 124	49	Polished White	31,418	29,304
K 124	49	Polished Bubinga	35,082	32,604
K 124	49	Polished Pyramid Mahogany	38,608	35,782
K 124	49	Satin Mahogany w/Vavona Inlay	31,647	29,510
K 124	49	Polished Mahogany w/Vavona Inlay	36,913	34,256

PIANOBUYER *Model & Price Supplement*

Model	Feet	Inches	Description	MSRP	SMP
HAESSLER *(continued)*					
K 124		49	Polished Burl Walnut	38,150	35,370
K 124		49	Satin Burl Walnut w/Walnut Inlay	31,647	29,510
K 124		49	Polished Burl Walnut w/Walnut Inlay	36,913	34,256
K 124		49	Satin Cherry and Yew	31,647	29,510
K 124		49	Polished Cherry and Yew	38,150	35,370
H 132		52	Polished Ebony	30,135	28,148
H 132		52	Satin Mahogany/Walnut	30,593	28,562
H 132		52	Polished Mahogany/Walnut	35,173	32,688
H 132		52	Satin Cherry	31,967	29,800
H 132		52	Polished Cherry	35,631	33,100
H 132		52	Polished White	32,425	30,212
H 132		52	Polished Bubinga	36,089	33,512
H 132		52	Palisander Rosewood	38,150	35,370
H 132		52	Polished Pyramid Mahogany	39,066	36,194
H 132		52	Satin Mahogany w/Vavona Inlay	33,570	31,244
H 132		52	Polished Mahogany w/Vavona Inlay	38,150	35,370
H 132		52	Polished Burl Walnut	38,150	35,370
H 132		52	Satin Burl Walnut w/Walnut Inlay	33,570	31,244
H 132		52	Polished Burl Walnut w/Walnut Inlay	38,150	35,370
H 132		52	Satin Cherry and Yew	33,570	31,244
H 132		52	Polished Cherry and Yew	38,150	35,370
K 132		52	Polished Ebony	33,204	30,914
K 132		52	Satin Mahogany/Walnut	33,662	31,326
K 132		52	Polished Mahogany/Walnut	38,242	35,452
K 132		52	Satin Cherry	35,036	32,564
K 132		52	Polished Cherry	38,700	35,864
K 132		52	Polished White	35,494	32,976
K 132		52	Polished Bubinga	39,158	36,278
K 132		52	Palisander Rosewood	41,219	38,134
K 132		52	Polished Pyramid Mahogany	42,134	38,958
K 132		52	Satin Mahogany w/Vavona Inlay	36,639	34,008
K 132		52	Polished Mahogany w/Vavona Inlay	41,219	38,134
K 132		52	Polished Burl Walnut	41,219	38,134
K 132		52	Satin Burl Walnut w/Walnut Inlay	36,639	34,008
K 132		52	Polished Burl Walnut w/Walnut Inlay	41,219	38,134
K 132		52	Satin Cherry and Yew	36,639	34,008
K 132		52	Polished Cherry and Yew	41,219	38,134
Grands					
H 175	5	8	Polished Ebony	78,239	71,486
H 175	5	8	Satin Mahogany/Walnut	84,107	76,772
H 175	5	8	Polished Mahogany/Walnut	92,010	83,892
H 175	5	8	Satin Cherry	83,403	76,138
H 175	5	8	Polished Cherry	94,162	85,830
H 175	5	8	Polished White	83,716	76,420

Model	Feet	Inches	Description	MSRP	SMP
HAESSLER (continued)					
H 175	5	8	Polished Bubinga	95,884	87,382
H 175	5	8	Palisander Rosewood	100,618	91,646
H 175	5	8	Polished Pyramid Mahogany	105,351	95,912
H 175	5	8	Polished Mahogany w/Vavona Inlay	115,250	104,828
H 175	5	8	Polished Burl Walnut	102,769	93,584
H 175	5	8	Polished Burl Walnut w/Walnut Inlay	115,250	104,828
H 175	5	8	Satin Cherry and Yew	109,225	99,400
H 175	5	8	Polished Cherry and Yew	115,250	104,828
H 175	5	8	Classic Alexandra Polished Ebony	92,822	84,624
H 175	5	8	Classic Alexandra Polished Walnut	106,460	96,910
H 175	5	8	Classic Alexandra Burl Walnut	117,114	106,508
H 175	5	8	Classic Alexandra Palisander	114,983	104,588
H 175	5	8	Louis XIV Satin White w/Gold	149,163	135,380
H 175	5	8	Satin and Polished Louis XV Mahogany	114,131	103,820
H 175	5	8	Ambassador Palisander	140,639	127,702
H 175	5	8	Ambassador Walnut	136,377	123,862
H 186	6	1	Polished Ebony	82,973	75,750
H 186	6	1	Satin Mahogany/Walnut	89,196	81,356
H 186	6	1	Polished Mahogany/Walnut	96,744	88,158
H 186	6	1	Satin Cherry	88,137	80,402
H 186	6	1	Polished Cherry	98,896	90,096
H 186	6	1	Polished White	88,781	80,982
H 186	6	1	Polished Bubinga	103,200	93,972
H 186	6	1	Palisander Rosewood	105,351	95,912
H 186	6	1	Polished Pyramid Mahogany	111,807	101,726
H 186	6	1	Polished Mahogany w/Vavona Inlay	119,984	109,094
H 186	6	1	Polished Burl Walnut	107,503	97,850
H 186	6	1	Polished Burl Walnut w/Walnut Inlay	119,984	109,094
H 186	6	1	Satin Cherry and Yew	104,491	95,136
H 186	6	1	Polished Cherry and Yew	119,984	109,094
H 186	6	1	Classic Alexandra Polished Ebony	97,510	88,846
H 186	6	1	Classic Alexandra Polished Walnut	111,147	101,132
H 186	6	1	Classic Alexandra Burl Walnut	121,802	110,732
H 186	6	1	Classic Alexandra Palisander	119,671	108,812
H 186	6	1	Louis XIV Satin White w/Gold	153,424	139,220
H 186	6	1	Satin and Polished Louis XV Mahogany	118,819	108,044
H 186	6	1	Ambassador Palisander	153,424	139,220
H 186	6	1	Ambassador Walnut	149,163	135,380
H 210	6	10	Polished Ebony	96,615	88,040
H 210	6	10	Satin Mahogany/Walnut	103,861	94,568
H 210	6	10	Polished Mahogany/Walnut	114,303	103,976
H 210	6	10	Satin Cherry	105,007	95,602
H 210	6	10	Polished Cherry	116,110	105,604
H 210	6	10	Polished White	103,378	94,134
H 210	6	10	Polished Bubinga	117,832	107,154
H 210	6	10	Palisander Rosewood	126,869	115,296

Model	Feet	Inches	Description	MSRP	SMP
HAESSLER *(continued)*					
H 210	6	10	Polished Pyramid Mahogany	133,325	121,112
H 210	6	10	Polished Mahogany w/Vavona Inlay	141,932	128,866
H 210	6	10	Polished Burl Walnut	124,718	113,358
H 210	6	10	Polished Burl Walnut w/Walnut Inlay	141,932	128,866
H 210	6	10	Satin Cherry and Yew	124,804	113,436
H 210	6	10	Polished Cherry and Yew	141,932	128,866
H 210	6	10	Classic Alexandra Polished Ebony	111,020	101,018
H 210	6	10	Classic Alexandra Polished Walnut	128,536	116,798
H 210	6	10	Classic Alexandra Burl Walnut	138,849	126,090
H 210	6	10	Classic Alexandra Palisander	140,980	128,010
H 210	6	10	Louis XIV Satin White w/Gold	187,519	169,936
H 210	6	10	Satin and Polished Louis XV Mahogany	132,329	120,214
H 210	6	10	Ambassador Palisander	166,210	150,738
H 210	6	10	Ambassador Walnut	161,948	146,900

HAILUN

Verticals

Model	Feet	Inches	Description	MSRP	SMP
HU116		45.5	Institutional Polished Ebony	10,308	7,246
HU1-P		48	Polished Ebony	11,135	7,670
HU1-P		48	Polished Mahogany/Walnut	11,998	8,290
HU1-PS		48	Polished Ebony with Nickel Trim	11,604	7,936
HU1-EP		48	Polished Ebony w/mahogany leg, fallboard, cheekblocks	12,038	8,190
HU121		48	Polished Ebony	7,950	6,500
HU121		48	Polished Mahogany	8,250	6,700
HU5-P		50	Polished Ebony	12,466	8,230
HU5-P		50	Polished Ebony with Nickel Trim	12,826	8,436
HU5-P		50	Polished Mahogany/Walnut	12,826	8,436
HU7-P		52	Polished Ebony w/Sostenuto	17,001	11,418

Grands

Model	Feet	Inches	Description	MSRP	SMP
HG150	4	10	Polished Ebony	16,485	12,390
HG150	4	10	Polished Mahogany	17,085	12,790
HG151	4	11.5	Polished Ebony	20,747	14,760
HG151	4	11.5	Polished Mahogany/Walnut	24,233	15,256
HG151C	4	11.5	Chippendale Polished Mahogany/Walnut	24,951	15,466
HG161	5	4	Polished Ebony	25,006	16,508
HG161	5	4	Polished Mahogany/Walnut	27,182	16,960
HG161G	5	4	Georgian Polished Mahogany/Walnut	30,151	17,760
HG178	5	10	Polished Ebony	30,024	19,416
HG178	5	10	Polished Mahogany/Walnut	31,338	20,284
HG178B	5	10	Baroque Polished Ebony w/Birds-Eye Maple Accents	33,605	20,480
HG198	6	5	Emerson Polished Ebony	46,689	28,760
HG198	6	5	Emerson Polished Mahogany/Walnut	49,112	29,494
HG218	7	2	Paulello Polished Ebony	65,210	38,812

Model	Feet	Inches	Description	MSRP	SMP

HALLET, DAVIS & CO.

Heritage Collection Verticals

Model	Feet	Inches	Description	MSRP	SMP
H108		43	Continental Polished Ebony	5,295	4,300
H108		43	Continental Polished Mahogany	5,495	4,390
H117H		46	Polished Ebony	5,950	4,500
H117H		46	Polished Mahogany	6,150	4,590
H118F		46	Demi-Chippendale Polished Ebony	5,995	4,700
H118F		46	Demi-Chippendale Polished Mahogany	6,195	4,790

Signature Collection Verticals

Model	Feet	Inches	Description	MSRP	SMP
HS109D		43	Continental Polished Ebony	5,695	4,500
HS109D		43	Continental Polished Mahogany	5,995	4,700
HS115M2		45	Classic Studio Polished Ebony	7,195	4,790
HS115M2		45	Classic Studio Polished Mahogany/Walnut/White	7,395	4,990
HS118M		46.5	Polished Ebony	7,595	5,190
HS118M		46.5	Polished Mahogany/Walnut/White	7,795	5,390
HS121S		48	Polished Ebony	8,795	5,590
HS121S		48	Polished Mahogany/Walnut/White	9,095	5,790
HS131Y		52	Polished Ebony	9,495	6,390

Heritage Collection Grands

Model	Feet	Inches	Description	MSRP	SMP
H142C	4	7	Polished Ebony	13,195	9,390
H142C	4	7	Polished Mahogany	13,995	9,790

Signature Collection Grands

Model	Feet	Inches	Description	MSRP	SMP
HS148	4	10	Satin Ebony	14,695	9,990
HS148	4	10	Polished Ebony	13,995	9,390
HS148	4	10	Polished Ebony w/Silver Plate	14,695	9,990
HS148	4	10	Polished Mahogany/Walnut/White	14,695	9,990
HS148	4	10	Polished White w/Silver Plate	15,395	10,590
HS160	5	3	Satin Ebony	15,995	10,990
HS160	5	3	Polished Ebony	15,395	10,390
HS160	5	3	Polished Ebony w/Silver Plate	15,995	10,990
HS160	5	3	Polished Mahogany/Walnut/White	15,995	10,990
HS170	5	7	Satin Ebony	16,995	12,190
HS170	5	7	Polished Ebony	16,495	11,590
HS170	5	7	Polished Mahogany/Walnut/White	16,995	12,190
HS188	6	2	Satin Ebony	20,495	14,590
HS188	6	2	Polished Ebony	19,995	13,990
HS188	6	2	Polished Mahogany/Walnut	20,495	14,590
HS212	7		Polished Ebony	29,995	26,990

HARDMAN, PECK & CO.

Performance Series Verticals

Model	Feet	Inches	Description	MSRP	SMP
R110S		44	Polished Ebony	5,495	4,310
R110S		44	Polished Mahogany	5,695	4,390

Model	Feet	Inches	Description	MSRP	SMP
HARDMAN, PECK & CO. *(continued)*					
R115LS		45	Polished Ebony	5,995	4,510
R115LS		45	Polished Mahogany	6,195	4,590
R116		46	School Polished Ebony	6,695	4,990
R116		46	School Satin Cherry	6,895	5,110
R117XK		46	Chippendale Polished Mahogany	6,695	4,910
R120LS		48	Polished Ebony	6,495	4,910
R120LS		48	Polished Mahogany	6,695	4,990
R132HA		52	Polished Ebony	9,495	6,490
Concert Series Verticals					
R110C		44	Polished Ebony	5,795	4,590
R110C		44	Polished Mahogany	5,995	4,790
R115GC		45	Polished Ebony	6,595	4,790
R115GC		45	Polished Mahogany	6,995	4,990
R123C		49	Polished Ebony	7,295	5,390
R123C		49	Polished Mahogany	7,595	5,590
Performance Series Grands					
R143S	4	8	Polished Ebony	13,895	9,390
R143S	4	8	Polished Mahogany	14,995	9,790
R143F	4	8	French Provincial Polished Mahogany	15,395	10,190
R150S	5		Polished Ebony	15,995	9,990
R158S	5	3	Polished Ebony	16,795	10,590
R158S	5	3	Polished Mahogany	17,495	10,990
R168S	5	7	Polished Ebony	18,195	11,390
R168S	5	7	Polished Mahogany	18,995	11,790
R185S	6	1	Polished Ebony	20,995	13,190
R185S	6	1	Polished Mahogany	22,395	13,790
Concert Series Grands					
R146C	4	10	Polished Ebony	14,595	9,390
R146C	4	10	Polished Mahogany	15,395	9,990
R165C	5	5	Polished Ebony	18,495	11,390
R165C	5	5	Polished Mahogany	19,495	11,990
R185S	6	1	Polished Mahogany	22,395	13,790
HEINTZMAN & CO.					
Heintzman Verticals					
121DL		48	Satin Mahogany	7,995	7,380
123B		48.5	Polished Mahogany	8,795	7,580
123F		48.5	French Provincial Polished Mahogany	7,995	6,980
126C		50	Polished Ebony	8,795	7,600
126 Royal		50	Polished Ebony	9,795	8,200
132D		52	Polished Mahogany, Decorative Panel	11,795	8,980

Model	Feet	Inches	Description	MSRP	SMP
HEINTZMAN & CO. *(continued)*					
132E		52	French Provincial Polished Ebony	11,795	8,780
132E		52	French Provincial Satin and Polished Mahogany	11,795	8,980
132 Royal		52	Satin Mahogany	12,795	9,580
140CK		55	Polished Mahogany	14,995	10,980
Gerhard Heintzman Verticals					
G118		47	Polished Ebony w/Silver Plate and Trim	4,995	4,995
G118		47	Polished Mahogany w/Silver Plate and Trim	5,195	5,195
G120		48	Polished Ebony w/Silver Plate and Trim	5,995	5,700
G120		48	Polished Mahogany w/Silver Plate and Trim	6,195	5,900
G126		50	Polished Ebony w/Silver Plate and Trim	7,995	6,400
G126		50	Polished Mahogany w/Silver Plate and Trim	8,195	6,600
G132		52	Polished Ebony w/Silver Plate and Trim	9,295	7,200
Heintzman Grands					
168	5	6	Polished Ebony	18,995	16,990
168	5	6	Polished Mahogany	19,995	17,390
168 Royal	5	6	Polished Ebony	23,995	17,990
186	6	1	Polished Ebony	21,995	18,980
186	6	1	Polished Mahogany	22,995	20,180
186 Royal	6	1	Polished Ebony	26,995	19,980
203	6	8	Polished Ebony	24,995	20,580
203 Royal	6	8	Polished Ebony	29,995	21,580
277	9		Polished Ebony	89,995	60,995
Gerhard Heintzman Grands					
G152	5		Polished Ebony	9,995	9,995
G152	5		Polished White	11,995	11,995
G152R	5		Empire Polished Mahogany	11,995	11,995
G168	5	6	Polished Ebony	15,995	12,800
G168	5	6	Polished White	19,995	13,800
G168R	5	6	Empire Polished Mahogany	17,995	13,800

Model	Feet	Inches	Description	MSRP	SMP
HOFFMANN, W.					
Vision Series Verticals					
V112		44.5	Polished Ebony	12,220	12,220
V112		44.5	Polished Mahogany/Walnut	14,180	14,180
V112		44.5	Polished White	14,180	14,180
V112		44.5	Chippendale Polished Maogany	15,720	15,720
V112		44.5	Chippendale Polished Walnut	15,720	14,042
V120		47.6	Polished Ebony	14,180	14,180
V120		47.6	Polished White	16,120	16,120
V120		47.6	Chippendale Polished Mahogany	17,680	17,150
V120		47.6	Chippendale Polished Walnut	17,680	15,364
V120		47.6	Rococo Satin White	18,640	18,640

Model	Feet	Inches	Description	MSRP	SMP

HOFFMANN, W. *(continued)*

Model	Feet	Inches	Description	MSRP	SMP
V120		47.6	Rococo Polished White	19,420	19,420
V126		49.6	Polished Ebony	16,120	16,120
V126		49.6	Polished White	17,860	17,860
V131		51.8	Polished Ebony	18,060	18,060

Tradition Series Verticals

T122		48	Polished Ebony	16,700	16,700
T122		48	Satin Mahogany/Walnut	19,220	19,220
T122		48	Polished Mahogany/Walnut	19,220	19,220
T122		48	Polished White	18,640	18,640
T128		50.4	Polished Ebony	18,060	18,060
T128		50.4	Satin Mahogany/Walnut	21,180	21,180
T128		50.4	Polished Mahogany/Walnut	21,180	21,180
T128		50.4	Polished White	20,000	20,000

Professional Series Verticals

P114		45	Polished Ebony w/Chrome Hardware	17,680	17,680
P114		45	Polished White w/Chrome Hardware	19,620	19,620
P120		47.2	Polished Ebony w/Chrome Hardware	18,840	18,840
P120		47.2	Polished White w/Chrome Hardware	20,780	20,780
P126		49.6	Polished Ebony w/Chrome Hardware	20,000	20,000

Vision Series Grands

V158	5	2	Polished Ebony	32,100	32,100
V158	5	2	Polished Mahogany/Walnut/White	35,980	35,980
V175	5	9	Polished Ebony	35,980	35,980
V175	5	9	Polished Walnut/Mahogany/White	39,880	39,880
V183	6		Polished Ebony	39,880	39,880
V183	6		Polished Walnut/Mahogany/White	43,760	43,760

Tradition Series Grands

T161	5	3	Polished Ebony	41,820	41,820
T161	5	3	Polished Mahogany/Walnut	47,660	47,660
T161	5	3	Polished White	45,720	45,720
T177	5	10	Polished Ebony	47,660	47,660
T177	5	10	Polished Mahogany/Walnut	53,480	53,480
T177	5	10	Polished White	51,540	51,540
T186	6	1	Polished Ebony	53,480	53,480
T186	6	1	Polished Mahogany/Walnut	59,320	59,320
T186	6	1	Polished White	57,380	57,380

Professional Series Grands

P162	5	4	Polished Ebony w/Chrome Hardware	52,980	52,980
P188	6	2	Polished Ebony w/Chrome Hardware	58,820	58,820
P206	6	9	Polished Ebony w/Chrome Hardware	66,600	66,600

Model	Feet	Inches	Description	MSRP	SMP

HUPFELD

Studio Edition Verticals

Model	Feet	Inches	Description	MSRP	SMP
HU 118		46.5	Polished Ebony	6,462	6,462
HU 121		47.5	Polished Ebony	6,725	6,725
HU 121		47.5	Polished White	6,865	6,865
HU 125		49	Polished Ebony	8,208	8,208
HU 132		52	Polished Ebony	9,563	9,500

Europe Edition Verticals

Model	Feet	Inches	Description	MSRP	SMP
HU 116E		45.5	Polished Ebony	11,086	10,854
HU 116E		45.5	Satin Mahogany/Walnut	11,086	10,854
HU 116E		45.5	Polished Mahogany/Walnut	11,782	11,473
HU 116E		45.5	Satin Cherry	11,782	11,473
HU 116E		45.5	Polished Cherry/White	13,174	12,710
HU 122E		48	Polished Ebony	12,304	11,937
HU 122E		48	Satin Mahogany/Walnut	12,304	11,937
HU 122E		48	Polished Mahogany/Walnut	13,000	12,556
HU 122E		48	Satin Cherry	13,000	12,556
HU 122E		48	Polished Cherry/White	14,392	13,793
HU 122E		48	Polished Bubinga	15,401	14,690
HU 132E		52	Polished Ebony	13,035	12,587
HU 132E		52	Satin Mahogany/Walnut	13,035	12,587
HU 132E		52	Polished Mahogany/Walnut	13,731	13,205
HU 132E		52	Satin Cherry	13,731	13,205
HU 132E		52	Polished Cherry/White	15,123	14,443
HU 132E		52	Polished Bubinga	18,185	17,164

Studio Edition Grands

Model	Feet	Inches	Description	MSRP	SMP
HU 148	4	10	Polished Ebony	17,989	16,990
HU 148	4	10	Polished Mahogany/Walnut	19,037	17,922
HU 148	4	10	Polished White	18,689	17,612
HU 160	5	3	Polished Ebony	20,783	19,474
HU 160	5	3	Polished Mahogany/Walnut	21,641	20,236
HU 160	5	3	Polished White	21,483	20,096
HU 188	6	2	Polished Ebony	29,691	27,392
HU 188	6	2	Polished Mahogany/Walnut	30,303	27,936
HU 188	6	2	Polished White	30,391	28,014
HU 213	7		Polished Ebony	36,329	33,292
HU 213	7		Polished White	38,075	34,844

Europe Edition Grands

Model	Feet	Inches	Description	MSRP	SMP
HU 160E	5	3	Polished Ebony	34,724	31,866
HU 160E	5	3	Polished Mahogany/Walnut	37,197	34,064
HU 160E	5	3	Polished Cherry/Bubinga/White	40,083	36,629
HU 175E	5	9	Polished Ebony	38,022	34,797
HU 175E	5	9	Polished Mahogany/Walnut	40,495	36,996

Model	Feet	Inches	Description	MSRP	SMP
HUPFELD *(continued)*					
HU 175E	5	9	Polished Bubinga/White	43,380	39,560
HU 186E	6	3	Polished Ebony	45,441	41,392
HU 186E	6	3	Polished Mahogany/Walnut	47,914	43,590
HU 186E	6	3	Polished Bubinga/White	50,799	46,155
HU 210E	6	10.5	Polished Ebony	50,799	46,155
HU 228E	7	6.5	Polished Ebony	59,043	53,483

IRMLER

Studio Edition Verticals

Model	Feet	Inches	Description	MSRP	SMP
P112		44	Polished Ebony	6,318	6,318
P118		46.5	Polished Ebony	6,576	6,573
P118		46.5	Polished White	6,712	6,688
P125		49	Polished Ebony	8,026	7,802

Art Design Verticals

Model	Feet	Inches	Description	MSRP	SMP
Mia		47.5	Polished Ebony	8,725	8,394
Gina		48.5	Polished Ebony	9,095	8,708
Monique		49	Polished Ebony	9,095	8,708
Louis		49	Polished Ebony	8,725	8,394
Titus		49	Polished Ebony	9,095	8,708
Alexa		49	Polished Ebony	10,320	9,746
Carlo		49	Polished Ebony	10,320	9,746

Supreme Edition Verticals

Model	Feet	Inches	Description	MSRP	SMP
SP118		46.5	Polished Ebony	8,169	7,923
SP121		48	Polished Ebony	8,725	8,394
SP125		49	Polished Ebony	9,579	9,118
SP132		52	Polished Ebony	10,622	10,002

Professional Edition Verticals

Model	Feet	Inches	Description	MSRP	SMP
P116E		46	Polished Ebony	9,362	8,934
P116E		46	Satin Mahogany/Walnut	9,362	8,934
P116E		46	Satin Cherry	9,949	9,431
P116E		46	Polished Mahogany/Walnut	9,949	9,431
P116E		46	Polished Cherry/White	11,125	10,428
P122E		48	Polished Ebony	10,390	9,805
P122E		48	Satin Mahogany/Walnut	10,390	9,805
P122E		48	Satin Cherry	10,978	10,303
P122E		48	Polished Mahogany/Walnut	10,978	10,303
P122E		48	Polished Cherry/White	12,153	11,299
P122E		48	Polished Bubinga	13,005	12,021
P132E		52	Polished Ebony	11,007	10,328
P132E		52	Satin Mahogany/Walnut	11,007	10,328
P132E		52	Satin Cherry	11,595	10,826
P132E		52	Polished Mahogany/Walnut	11,595	10,826

Model	Feet	Inches	Description	MSRP	SMP
IRMLER (continued)					
P132E		52	Polished Cherry/White	12,770	11,822
P132E		52	Polished Bubinga	15,356	14,014
Studio Edition Grands					
F148	4	10	Polished Ebony	17,589	15,906
F148	4	10	Polished Mahogany/Walnut	18,614	16,775
F148	4	10	Polished White	18,273	16,486
F160	5	3	Polished Ebony	20,321	18,221
F160	5	3	Polished Mahogany/Walnut	21,160	18,932
F160	5	3	Polished White	21,006	18,802
F188	6	2	Polished Ebony	29,031	25,603
F188	6	2	Polished Mahogany/Walnut	29,630	26,110
F188	6	2	Polished White	29,715	26,182
F213	7		Polished Ebony	35,521	31,103
F213	7		Polished White	37,228	32,549
Professional Edition Grands					
F160E	5	3	Polished Ebony	32,409	28,465
F160E	5	3	Polished Mahogany/Walnut	34,718	30,422
F160E	5	3	Polished Cherry	37,410	32,703
F160E	5	3	Polished White	37,410	32,703
F160E	5	3	Polished Bubinga	37,410	32,703
F175E	5	9	Polished Ebony	35,487	31,074
F175E	5	9	Polished Mahogany/Walnut	37,795	33,030
F175E	5	9	Polished White	40,488	35,312
F175E	5	9	Polished Bubinga	40,488	35,312
F190E	6	3	Polished Ebony	42,412	36,942
F190E	6	3	Polished Mahogany/Walnut	44,720	38,898
F190E	6	3	Polished White	47,413	41,181
F190E	6	3	Polished Bubinga	47,413	41,181
F210E	6	10.5	Polished Ebony	47,413	41,181
F230E	7	6.5	Polished Ebony	55,107	47,701

KAWAI

Verticals

Model	Feet	Inches	Description	MSRP	SMP
K-15		44	Continental Polished Ebony	5,895	5,690
K-15		44	Continental Polished Mahogany	6,095	5,890
K-15		44	Continental Polished Snow White	6,195	5,990
506N		44.5	Satin Ebony/Mahogany	5,895	5,690
508		44.5	Satin Mahogany	6,695	6,390
607		44.5	French Renaissance Satin Cherry	7,995	7,390
607		44.5	Queen Anne Satin Mahogany	7,995	7,390
K-200		45	Satin and Polished Ebony	7,995	7,390
K-200		45	Satin and Polished Mahogany	8,695	7,990
K-200NKL		45	Satin and Polished Ebony with Nickel Trim	8,395	7,690

Model	Feet	Inches	Description	MSRP	SMP
KAWAI (*continued*)					
UST-9		46	Satin Ebony/Oak/Walnut/Cherry	7,995	7,590
ST-1		46	Satin Ebony/Oak/Walnut/Cherry	8,695	7,990
907N		46.5	English Regency Satin Mahogany	10,695	9,990
907N		46.5	French Provincial Satin Cherry	10,695	9,990
K-300		48	Satin and Polished Ebony	12,095	10,790
K-300		48	Satin and Polished Mahogany	12,895	11,290
K-300		48	Polished Snow White	13,095	11,490
K-300NKL		48	Satin and Polished Ebony with Nickel Trim	12,495	10,990
K-400		48	Polished Ebony	12,895	11,290
K-400NKL		48	Polished Ebony with Nickel Trim	13,195	11,590
K-500		51	Satin and Polished Ebony	15,695	13,590
K-500		51	Polished Sapele Mahogany	17,695	15,190
K-800		53	Polished Ebony	24,995	20,990

AnyTime (Silent) Verticals

Model	Feet	Inches	Description	MSRP	SMP
K-200 ATX3-CA		45	AnyTime Polished Ebony w/CA Sound	12,495	10,990
K-300 AURES		48	AnyTime Polished Ebony w/Soundboard Speaker	17,495	14,990

Grands

Model	Feet	Inches	Description	MSRP	SMP
GL-10	5		Satin and Polished Ebony	16,295	15,190
GL-10	5		Polished Ebony with Nickel Trim	17,195	15,990
GL-10	5		Polished Mahogany/Snow White	17,895	16,590
GL-10	5		French Provincial Polished Mahogany	18,995	17,590
GL-20	5	2	Satin and Polished Ebony	21,195	20,390
GL-20	5	2	Polished Sapele Mahogany	25,395	23,390
GL-20	5	2	Polished Snow White	24,495	22,590
GL-30	5	5	Satin and Polished Ebony	29,295	26,790
GL-30	5	5	Polished Sapele Mahogany	35,195	31,990
GL-30	5	5	Satin Dark Walnut	35,195	31,990
GL-30	5	5	Polished Snow White	33,995	30,790
GX-1 BLK	5	5	Satin and Polished Ebony	39,495	32,590
GX-1 BLK	5	5	Polished Dark Walnut	45,995	37,790
GL-40	5	11	Satin and Polished Ebony	34,495	31,390
GL-40	5	11	Polished Sapele Mahogany	40,895	36,990
GL-40	5	11	Satin Dark Walnut	40,895	36,990
GX-2 BLK	5	11	Satin and Polished Ebony	45,495	37,390
GX-2 BLK	5	11	Satin Walnut/Cherry/Oak	50,495	41,390
GX-2 BLK	5	11	Polished Walnut/Sapeli Mahogany	52,495	42,990
GX-2 BLK	5	11	Polished Snow White	48,495	39,790
CR40-PL	6	1	Plexiglass Crystal Piano	231,495	186,190
GL-50	6	2	Polished Ebony	39,795	35,990
GX-3 BLK	6	2	Satin and Polished Ebony	58,495	47,790
GX-5 BLK	6	7	Satin and Polished Ebony	66,195	53,990
GX-6 BLK	7		Satin and Polished Ebony	74,195	60,390
GX-7 BLK	7	6	Satin and Polished Ebony	85,195	69,790
EX-L	9	1	Polished Ebony	234,695	188,790

Acoustic Piano Model & Pricing Guide

Model	Feet	Inches	Description	MSRP	SMP

KAWAI (continued)
AnyTime (Silent) Grands

Model	Feet	Inches	Description	MSRP	SMP
GL-30 ATX2-SS	5	5	AnyTime Polished Ebony w/Soundboard Speaker	32,295	29,390

KAWAI, SHIGERU
Grands

Model	Feet	Inches	Description	MSRP	SMP
SK-2	5	11	Polished Ebony	68,495	55,800
SK-2	5	11	Polished Sapele Mahogany	78,995	64,200
SK-3	6	2	Polished Ebony	79,995	65,000
SK-3	6	2	Polished Sapele Mahogany	91,995	74,600
SK-3	6	2	Polished Pyramid Mahogany	106,495	86,200
SK-5	6	7	Polished Ebony	92,295	74,800
SK-6	7		Polished Ebony	103,995	84,200
SK-7	7	6	Polished Ebony	115,295	93,200
SK-EX	9	1	Polished Ebony	256,495	206,200

KAYSERBURG
Verticals

Model	Feet	Inches	Description	MSRP	SMP
KA-121B		48	Polished Ebony	15,995	12,990
KA-121B		48	Polished Dark Walnut	16,995	13,790
KA-126B		50	Polished Ebony	18,495	14,590
KA-126B		50	Polished Cherry	19,995	15,390
KA-132B		52	Polished Ebony	20,995	16,190
KA-132C		52	Polished Ebony w/Sostenuto	21,495	16,990

Grands

Model	Feet	Inches	Description	MSRP	SMP
KA-180	5	11	Polished Ebony	59,995	52,990

KINGSBURG
Verticals

Model	Feet	Inches	Description	MSRP	SMP
LM 116		46	Chippendale Polished Walnut	6,610	5,893
KG 120		48	Polished Ebony	9,459	7,326
KU 120		48	Polished Ebony	8,815	6,114
KU 120		48	Satin and Polished Mahogany/Walnut	9,146	6,334
KG 122		48	Polished Ebony	10,085	7,657
KF 122		48	Polished Ebony	13,473	9,440
KF 123		50	Polished White & Red	13,480	9,862
KG 123		50	Decorator Satin Walnut	12,402	9,321
KU 123		50	Decorator Satin Walnut	9,917	6,996
KG 125		50	Polished Ebony	10,367	7,998
KU 125		50	Polished Ebony	9,917	6,775
KU 125		50	Polished Ebony w/Inlay	10,602	7,216

Model	Feet	Inches	Description	MSRP	SMP
KINGSBURG (continued)					
KU 125		50	Satin and Polished Mahogany/Walnut	10,469	6,996
KF 126		50	Satin Walnut	14,720	10,744
KF 128		50	Polished Ebony	14,498	11,626
KF 133		52	Polished Ebony	16,483	12,508
KG 133		52	Polished Ebony	12,497	9,421
KU 133		52	Polished Ebony	10,574	7,437
KU 133		52	Polished Mahogany/Walnut	11,003	7,657
Grands					
KF 158	5	3	Polished Ebony	25,909	25,859
KG 158	5	3	Polished Ebony	19,840	13,611
KG 158	5	3	Polished Ebony w/Inlay	20,942	14,272
KG 158	5	3	Polished Mahogany/Walnut	20,391	14,052
KG 175	5	9	Polished Ebony	22,320	14,006
KF 185	6	1	Polished Ebony	33,020	32,970
KG 185	6	1	Polished Ebony	24,250	15,375
KG 185	6	1	Polished Ebony w/Inlay	25,904	16,036
KG 185	6	1	Polished Mahogany/Walnut	25,352	15,816
KF 228	7	4	Polished Ebony	69,458	64,195

KNABE, WM.
Baltimore Series Verticals

Model	Feet	Inches	Description	MSRP	SMP
WV 43		43	Continental Polished Ebony	7,295	5,398
WV 243F		43	French Provincial Satin Cherry	7,995	5,798
WV 243T		43	Satin Mahogany/Walnut	7,995	5,798
WV 115		45	Satin Ebony	8,795	6,298
WV 115		45	Polished Ebony	7,995	5,798
WV 118H		46.5	Satin Ebony	9,295	6,598
WV 118H		46.5	Polished Ebony	8,995	6,398
Verticals			Other finishes, add		1,500

Academy Series Verticals

Model	Feet	Inches	Description	MSRP	SMP
WMV 245		45	Satin Ebony	8,695	6,198
WMV 245		45	Polished Ebony	8,295	5,998
WMV 247		46.5	Satin Ebony	9,995	6,998
WMV 247		46.5	Polished Ebony	9,695	6,798
WMV 647F		46.5	French Provincial Satin Cherry	9,695	6,798
WMV 647R		46.5	Renaissance Satin Walnut	9,695	6,798
WMV 647T		46.5	Satin Mahogany	9,695	6,798
WMV 121M		47.5	Satin Ebony	9,995	6,998
WMV 121M		47.5	Polished Ebony	9,695	6,798
WMV 132		52	Satin Ebony	12,295	8,398
WMV 132		52	Polished Ebony	11,695	7,998
Verticals			Other finishes, add		1,500

Acoustic Piano Model & Pricing Guide

Model	Feet	Inches	Description	MSRP	SMP

KNABE, WM. *(continued)*

Concert Artist Series Verticals

Model	Feet	Inches	Description	MSRP	SMP
WKV 118F		46.5	French Provincial Lacquer Semigloss Cherry	13,995	9,398
WKV 118R		46.5	Renaissance Lacquer Satin Ebony	13,995	9,398
WKV 118R		46.5	Renaissance Lacquer Semigloss Walnut	13,995	9,398
WKV 118T		46.5	Lacquer Semigloss Mahogany	13,995	9,398
WKV 121		48	Satin Ebony	14,595	9,798
WKV 121		48	Polished Ebony	13,995	9,398
WKV 132MD		52	Satin Ebony	15,995	10,598
WKV 132MD		52	Polished Ebony	14,595	9,798
Verticals			Other finishes, add		1,500

Baltimore Series Grands

Model	Feet	Inches	Description	MSRP	SMP
WG 50	5		Satin Ebony	18,295	11,998
WG 50	5		Polished Ebony	17,295	11,398
WG 50	5		Polished Mahogany/Walnut	18,595	12,198
WG 54	5	4	Satin Ebony	19,995	12,998
WG 54	5	4	Polished Ebony	18,595	12,198
WG 54	5	4	Polished Mahogany/Walnut	20,295	13,198
WG 54	5	4	Polished Ebony w/Bubinga or Pommele Accents	23,295	14,998
WSG 54	5	4	M Leg w/Bubinga or Pommele Accents	26,595	16,998
WG 59	5	9	Satin Ebony	24,695	15,798
WG 59	5	9	Polished Ebony	22,995	14,798
WG 61	6	1	Satin Ebony	25,995	16,598
WG 61	6	1	Polished Ebony	24,695	15,798
Grands			Other finishes, add		2,000

Academy Series Grands

Model	Feet	Inches	Description	MSRP	SMP
WMG 610	5	9	Satin Ebony	27,695	17,598
WMG 610	5	9	Polished Ebony	26,295	16,798
WMG 660	6	1	Satin Ebony	30,995	19,598
WMG 660	6	1	Polished Ebony	29,695	18,798
WFM 700T	6	10	Satin Ebony	33,995	21,398
WFM 700T	6	10	Polished Ebony	32,695	20,598
Grands			Other finishes, add		2,000

Concert Artist Series Grands

Model	Feet	Inches	Description	MSRP	SMP
WKG 53	5	3	Satin Ebony	33,295	20,998
WKG 53	5	3	Polished Ebony	32,295	20,398
WKG 58	5	8	Satin Ebony	40,995	25,598
WKG 58	5	8	Polished Ebony	39,995	24,998
WKG 70	7		Satin Ebony	56,295	34,798
WKG 70	7		Polished Ebony	55,295	34,198
WKG 76	7	6	Satin Ebony	58,195	35,898
WKG 76	7	6	Polished Ebony	57,295	35,398
WKG 90	9	2	Satin Ebony	147,595	89,598
WKG 90	9	2	Polished Ebony	143,595	87,198
Grands			Other finishes, add		2,000

Model	Feet	Inches	Description	MSRP	SMP
MASON & HAMLIN					
Verticals					
50		50	Satin and Polished Ebony	28,210	25,881
Verticals			Cambridge Collection, add	3,061	2,700
Grands					
B	5	4	Satin and Polished Ebony	62,802	53,314
B	5	4	Polished Mahogany/Walnut	67,120	56,911
B	5	4	Polished Pyramid Mahogany	76,624	64,828
B	5	4	Polished Rosewood	70,431	59,669
B	5	4	Polished Bubinga	73,035	61,838
B	5	4	Polished Macassar Ebony	76,624	64,828
A	5	8	Satin and Polished Ebony	72,334	61,255
A	5	8	Polished Mahogany/Walnut	77,132	65,252
A	5	8	Polished Pyramid Mahogany	93,653	79,013
A	5	8	Polished Rosewood	85,515	72,233
A	5	8	Polished Bubinga	88,508	74,727
A	5	8	Polished Macassar Ebony	93,653	79,013
AA	6	4	Satin and Polished Ebony	82,566	69,779
AA	6	4	Polished Mahogany/Walnut	87,025	73,493
AA	6	4	Polished Pyramid Mahogany	99,996	84,297
AA	6	4	Polished Rosewood	91,836	77,500
AA	6	4	Polished Bubinga	94,823	79,989
AA	6	4	Polished Macassar Ebony	99,996	84,297
BB	7		Satin and Polished Ebony	93,694	79,047
BB	7		Polished Mahogany/Walnut	97,009	81,810
BB	7		Polished Pyramid Mahogany	115,504	97,215
BB	7		Polished Rosewood	108,595	91,460
BB	7		Polished Bubinga	111,289	93,704
BB	7		Polished Macassar Ebony	115,504	97,215
CC	9	4	Satin and Polished Ebony	139,302	117,039
CC	9	4	Polished Mahogany/Walnut	149,104	125,204
CC	9	4	Polished Pyramid Mahogany	169,752	142,404
CC	9	4	Polished Rosewood	157,581	132,266
CC	9	4	Polished Bubinga	162,863	136,665
CC	9	4	Polished Macassar Ebony	169,752	142,404
Grands			Monticello Art Case, add	8,000	6,800
Grands			Cambridge Collection, add	8,000	6,800
PALATINO					
Verticals					
PUP-22C		48	Polished Mahogany/Cherry	5,000	5,000
PUP-22C		48	Satin Walnut	5,000	5,000
PUP-123T		48	Torino Polished Ebony	5,900	5,900
PUP-123T		48	Torino Polished Dark Walnut	6,200	6,200

Model	Feet	Inches	Description	MSRP	SMP
PALATINO (*continued*)					
PUP-125		50	Satin and Polished Ebony	5,950	5,950
PUP-125		50	Polished Mahogany/White	5,950	5,950
PUP-126		50	Capri Polished Ebony	6,900	6,900
PUP-126		50	Capri Polished Dark Walnut	7,500	7,500
Grands					
PGD-50	5		Milano Polished Ebony	12,000	12,000
PGD-50	5		Milano Polished Dark Walnut	12,500	12,500
PGD-59	5	9	Roma Polished Ebony	13,400	13,400
PGD-62	6	2	Firenze Polished Ebony	15,400	15,400

PEARL RIVER

Verticals

Model	Feet	Inches	Description	MSRP	SMP
EU 110		43	Polished Ebony	4,695	4,500
EU 110 Silent		43	Polished Ebony w/Silent System	7,995	6,900
EU 111PA		43	French Provincial Satin Cherry	5,995	5,300
EU 111PB		43	Mediterranean Satin Walnut	5,995	5,300
EU 111PC		43	Italian Provincial Satin Mahogany	5,995	5,300
UP 115E		45	Satin Ebony/Mahogany (School)	5,995	5,300
UP 115M5		45	Polished Ebony	4,995	4,700
UP 115M5		45	Polished Mahogany/Walnut/White	5,395	4,900
EU 118S		46.5	Polished Ebony w/Silver Hardware	5,595	5,190
EU 118S		46.5	Polished Mahogany/Walnut w/Silver Hardware	5,795	5,390
EU 122		48	Polished Ebony	6,695	5,790
EU 122		48	Polished Mahogany/Walnut/White	6,895	5,990
EU 122		48	Satin Cherry	6,895	5,990
EU 122S		48	Polished Ebony w/Silver Hardware	6,895	5,990
EU 122 Silent		48	Polished Ebony w/Silent System	9,195	8,190
EU 131		52	Polished Ebony	7,695	6,390

Grands

Model	Feet	Inches	Description	MSRP	SMP
GP 150	4	11	Hand-rubbed Satin Ebony	12,495	9,790
GP 150	4	11	Polished Ebony	11,995	9,390
GP 150	4	11	Polished Mahogany/Walnut/White	12,495	9,790
GP 150	4	11	Polished Sapele Mahogany/Artisan Walnut	12,995	10,190
GP 150SP	4	11	Polished Ebony w/Silver Plate/Hardware	12,495	9,790
GP 160	5	3	Hand-rubbed Satin Ebony	13,995	10,590
GP 160	5	3	Polished Ebony	13,495	10,190
GP 160	5	3	Polished Mahogany/Walnut/White	13,995	10,590
GP 160	5	3	Polished Sapele Mahogany/Artisan Walnut	13,995	10,990
GP 170	5	7	Hand-rubbed Satin Ebony	16,495	12,190
GP 170	5	7	Polished Ebony	15,995	11,790
GP 170	5	7	Polished Mahogany/Walnut	16,495	12,190
GP 170	5	7	Polished Sapele Mahogany/Artisan Walnut	16,995	12,590
GP 188A	6	2	Polished Ebony	18,995	14,390

Model	Feet	Inches	Description	MSRP	SMP

PEARL RIVER *(continued)*

Model	Feet	Inches	Description	MSRP	SMP
GP 212	7		Polished Ebony	30,995	23,990
GP 275	9		Polished Ebony	79,995	60,990

PERZINA
Verticals

Model	Feet	Inches	Description	MSRP	SMP
GP-112 Kompact		45	Continental Polished Ebony	8,890	8,000
GP-112 Kompact		45	Continental Polished Walnut/Mahogany	9,450	8,250
GP-112 Kompact		45	Continental Polished White	9,780	8,490
GP-115 Merit		45	Polished Ebony	9,660	8,430
GP-115 Merit		45	Polished Mahogany/Walnut	10,220	8,690
GP-115 Merit		45	Polished White	10,550	8,900
GP-115 Merit		45	Queen Anne Polished Ebony	10,220	8,600
GP-115 Merit		45	Queen Anne Polished Mahogany/Walnut	11,045	8,920
GP-115 Merit		45	Queen Anne Polished White	11,375	9,140
GP-122 Konsumat		48	Polished Ebony	10,990	9,090
GP-122 Konsumat		48	Polished Ebony with Chrome Hardware	12,090	10,000
GP-122 Konsumat		48	Polished Mahogany/Walnut	11,375	9,400
GP-122 Konsumat		48	Polished White	11,580	9,590
GP-122 Konsumat		48	Queen Anne Polished Ebony	11,375	9,380
GP-122 Konsumat		48	Queen Anne Polished Mahogany/Walnut	12,200	9,590
GP-122 Konsumat		48	Queen Anne Polished White	12,500	9,800
GP-122 Balmoral		48	Designer Polished Ebony	12,285	9,300
GP-122 Balmoral		48	Designer Polished Ebony/Bubinga (two-tone)	13,300	10,840
GP-129 Kapitol		51	Polished Ebony	12,240	10,220
GP-129 Kapitol		51	Polished Mahogany/Walnut	12,860	10,420
GP-129 Kapitol		51	Polished White	13,520	10,630
GP-129 Kapitol		51	Queen Anne Polished Ebony	13,520	10,420
GP-129 Kapitol		51	Queen Anne Polished Mahogany/Walnut	13,565	10,630
GP-129 Kapitol		51	Queen Anne Polished White	14,290	10,840
GP-130 Konzert		51	Polished Ebony	14,840	11,460

Grands

Model	Feet	Inches	Description	MSRP	SMP
GBT-152 Prysm	5	1	Polished Ebony	22,570	16,440
GBT-152 Prysm	5	1	Polished Mahogany/Walnut	24,680	17,650
GBT-152 Prysm	5	1	Polished White	26,750	17,860
GBT-152 Prysm	5	1	Designer Polished Ebony/Bubinga (two-tone)	28,620	18,480
GBT-152 Prysm	5	1	Designer Polished Mahogany/Walnut with Burled Walnut Inlay	29,920	19,520
GBT-152 Prysm	5	1	Designer Queen Anne or Empire Polished Ebony	23,090	16,760
GBT-152 Prysm	5	1	Designer Queen Anne or Empire Polished Mahogany/Walnut	25,160	17,980
GBT-152 Prysm	5	1	Designer Queen Anne or Empire Polished White	27,260	18,180
GBT-160 Sylvr	5	5	Polished Ebony	29,360	18,690
GBT-160 Sylvr	5	5	Polished Mahogany/Walnut	31,460	19,850

PERZINA (continued)

Model	Feet	Inches	Description	MSRP	SMP
GBT-160 Sylvr	5	5	Polished White	33,590	20,020
GBT-160 Sylvr	5	5	Designer Polished Ebony/Bubinga (two-tone)	37,610	23,900
GBT-160 Sylvr	5	5	Designer Polished Mahogany/Walnut with Burled Walnut Inlay	38,930	24,930
GBT-160 Sylvr	5	5	Designer Queen Anne or Empire Polished Ebony	30,330	19,020
GBT-160 Sylvr	5	5	Designer Queen Anne or Empire Polished Mahogany/Walnut	32,500	20,170
GBT-160 Sylvr	5	5	Designer Queen Anne or Empire Polished White	34,670	20,320
GBT-175 Granit	5	10	Polished Ebony	31,940	19,640
GBT-175 Granit	5	10	Polished Mahogany/Walnut	34,720	20,790
GBT-175 Granit	5	10	Polished White	37,160	20,980
GBT-175 Granit	5	10	Designer Polished Ebony/Bubinga (two-tone)	40,190	24,840
GBT-175 Granit	5	10	Designer Polished Mahogany/Walnut with Burled Walnut Inlay	41,300	25,880
GBT-175 Granit	5	10	Designer Queen Anne or Empire Polished Ebony	32,660	19,960
GBT-175 Granit	5	10	Designer Queen Anne or Empire Polished Mahogany/Walnut	35,340	21,120
GBT-175 Granit	5	10	Designer Queen Anne or Empire Polished White	38,810	21,300
GBT-187 Royal	6	2	Polished Ebony	35,770	20,590
GBT-187 Royal	6	2	Polished Mahogany/Walnut	37,270	21,750
GBT-187 Royal	6	2	Polished White	39,910	21,930
GBT-187 Royal	6	2	Designer Polished Ebony/Bubinga (two-tone)	44,020	25,780
GBT-187 Royal	6	2	Designer Polished Mahogany/Walnut with Burled Walnut Inlay	45,650	26,820
GBT-187 Royal	6	2	Designer Queen Anne or Empire Polished Ebony	36,720	20,910
GBT-187 Royal	6	2	Designer Queen Anne or Empire Polished Mahogany/Walnut	37,940	22,070
GBT-187 Royal	6	2	Designer Queen Anne or Empire Polished White	40,350	22,250

PETROF

Most models are also available in finishes other than those shown here.

Verticals

Model	Inches	Description	MSRP	SMP
P 118 C1	46.25	Chippendale Polished Ebony	28,258	20,824
P 118 D1	46.25	Demi-Chippendale Polished Ebony	27,530	20,294
P 118 G2	46.25	Polished Ebony	26,794	19,760
P 118 M1	46.25	Polished Ebony	25,504	18,820
P 118 P1	46.25	Polished Ebony	24,980	18,440
P 118 R1	46.25	Rococo Satin White w/Gold Trim	29,930	22,046
P 118 S1	46.25	Continental Polished Ebony/White	21,968	16,250
P 122 N1	47.75	Polished Ebony	26,100	19,240
P 125 F1	49.25	Polished Ebony	26,990	19,900
P 125 G1	49.25	Polished Ebony	28,490	20,990
P 125 M1	49.25	Polished Ebony	28,090	20,700
P 127 NEXT	49.5	Satin Ebony with Chrome Legs	39,540	29,030
P 127 NEXT	49.5	Satin Wood Tones with Chrome Legs	43,790	32,120

Model	Feet	Inches	Description	MSRP	SMP
PETROF *(continued)*					
P 131 M1		51	Polished Ebony	38,570	28,326
P 135 K1		53	Polished Ebony	45,980	33,714
Grands					
P 159	5	2	Bora Polished Ebony	75,910	55,480
P 159	5	2	Bora Demi-Chippendale Polished Ebony	81,990	58,778
P 173	5	6	Breeze Polished Ebony	79,990	58,448
P 173	5	6	Breeze Chippendale Polished Ebony	90,958	68,424
P 173	5	6	Breeze Demi-Chippendale Polished Ebony	88,700	68,780
P 173	5	6	Breeze Klasik Polished Ebony	89,240	70,776
P 173	5	6	Breeze Rococo Satin White w/Gold Trim	94,190	68,780
P 194	6	3	Storm Polished Ebony	83,964	61,336
P 194	6	3	Storm Styl Polished Ebony	96,060	70,136
P 210	6	10	Pasat Polished Ebony	119,990	87,500
P 237	7	9	Monsoon Polished Ebony	157,390	120,740
P 284	9	2	Mistral Polished Ebony	217,084	158,152
Grands			Mahogany/Walnut Upcharge	2,400	2,400
Grands			White or Color Upcharge	1,600	1,600

PRAMBERGER

Legacy Series Verticals

Model	Feet	Inches	Description	MSRP	SMP
LV-110		43	Continental Polished Ebony	7,495	5,498
LV-43F		43	French Provincial Satin Cherry	8,095	5,898
LV-43T		43	Satin Mahogany/Walnut	8,095	5,898
LV-115		45	Satin Ebony	8,795	6,298
LV-115		45	Polished Ebony	8,095	5,898
LV-115		45	Polished Mahogany/Walnut	8,995	6,398
LV-118		46.5	Satin Ebony	9,495	6,698
LV-118		46.5	Polished Ebony	8,795	6,298

Signature Series Verticals

Model	Feet	Inches	Description	MSRP	SMP
PV-118F/R/T		46.5	Decorator Satin Cherry/Mahogany/Walnut	9,995	6,998
PV-118S		46.5	Satin Ebony	10,295	7,198
PV-118S		46.5	Polished Ebony	9,695	6,798
PV-121		47.5	Satin Ebony	11,695	7,998
PV-121		47.5	Polished Ebony	10,995	7,598
PV-132		52	Satin Ebony	12,995	8,798
PV-132		52	Polished Ebony	12,299	8,398

J.P. Pramberger Platinum Series Verticals

Model	Feet	Inches	Description	MSRP	SMP
JP-132		52	Satin Ebony	16,295	10,798
JP-132		52	Polished Ebony	14,995	9,998
Verticals			Other wood finishes, add		1,500

Legacy Series Grands

Model	Feet	Inches	Description	MSRP	SMP
LG-150	5		Satin Ebony	18,295	11,998
LG-150	5		Polished Ebony	17,295	11,398

Model	Feet	Inches	Description	MSRP	SMP
PRAMBERGER (continued)					
LG-150	5		Polished Mahogany/Walnut	18,595	24,998
LG-157	5	2	Satin Ebony	19,995	12,798
LG-157	5	2	Polished Ebony	18,595	11,998
LG-157	5	2	Polished Ebony w/Bubinga or Pommele Accents	23,295	14,198
LG-157	5	2	Polished Fire Red	24,995	15,198
LG-175	5	9	Satin Ebony	24,595	14,598
LG-175	5	9	Polished Ebony	22,995	13,798
Signature Series Grands					
PS-157	5	2	Satin Ebony	24,695	15,198
PS-157	5	2	Polished Ebony	23,295	14,398
PS-157	5	2	Polished Ebony w/Bubinga or Pommele Accents	27,295	16,598
PS-175	5	9	Satin Ebony	26,695	16,398
PS-175	5	9	Polished Ebony	25,295	15,598
PS-185	6	1	Satin Ebony	27,695	16,998
PS-185	6	1	Polished Ebony	26,295	16,198
PS-208	6	10	Satin Ebony	34,995	21,798
PS-208	6	10	Polished Ebony	33,295	20,598
J.P. Pramberger Platinum Series Grands					
JP-179L	5	10	Satin Ebony	42,795	24,998
JP-179L	5	10	Polished Ebony	41,595	24,398
JP-179LF	5	10	French Provincial Satin Ebony	49,995	28,998
JP-179LF	5	10	French Provincial Lacquer Semigloss Cherry	49,995	28,998
JP-208B	6	10	Satin Ebony	54,295	31,398
JP-208B	6	10	Polished Ebony	53,195	30,798
JP-228C	7	6	Satin Ebony	59,095	34,198
JP-228C	7	6	Polished Ebony	58,495	33,798
JP-280E	9	2	Polished Ebony	174,595	98,998
Grands			Other wood finishes, add		2,000

RITMÜLLER

Classic Verticals

Model	Feet	Inches	Description	MSRP	SMP
UP 110RB		43	French Provincial Satin Cherry	6,995	5,390
UP 110RB1		43	Italian Provincial Satin Walnut	6,995	5,390
UP 120RE		47.25	Satin Mahogany	8,195	6,190
UP 121RB		47.6	Polished Ebony	7,195	5,990
UP 121RB		47.6	Polished Mahogany/Walnut/White	7,695	6,190

Performance Verticals

Model	Feet	Inches	Description	MSRP	SMP
R1		47	Polished Ebony	8,595	6,790
R2		49	Polished Ebony w/Butterfly Lid	9,595	7,390
RB		49	Polished Ebony	9,595	7,390

Model	Feet	Inches	Description	MSRP	SMP

RITMÜLLER (continued)

Premium Verticals

Model	Feet	Inches	Description	MSRP	SMP
UH 121R		48	Chippendale Polished Ebony	10,095	8,100
UH 121R		48	Chippendale Polished Sapele Mahogany	10,495	8,390
UH 121RA		48	Polished Ebony	9,995	7,990
UH 121RA Silent		48	Polished Ebony w/Silent System	13,495	10,390
UH 132R		52	Polished Ebony	12,195	9,190

Performance Grands

Model	Feet	Inches	Description	MSRP	SMP
R8	4	11	Polished Ebony	14,195	10,190
R8	4	11	Polished Ebony w/Silver Plate/Hardware	14,495	10,790
R8	4	11	Polished Mahogany/White	14,495	10,790
R9	5	3	Polished Ebony	15,695	10,990
R9	5	3	Polished Mahogany/White	16,195	11,590

Premium Grands

Model	Feet	Inches	Description	MSRP	SMP
GH 148R	4	10	Polished Ebony	16,495	11,990
GH 148R	4	10	Polished Sapele Mahogany	16,995	12,790
GH 160R	5	3	Hand-rubbed Satin Ebony	19,495	14,790
GH 160R	5	3	Polished Ebony	18,995	13,990
GH 160R	5	3	Polished Sapele Mahogany	19,495	14,790
GH 160RA	5	3	Polished Ebony (round leg)	19,495	14,790
GH 170R	5	7	Polished Ebony	21,495	16,390
GH 188R	6	2	Polished Ebony	26,495	19,990
GH 212R	7		Polished Ebony	32,995	26,990
GH 275R	9		Polished Ebony	84,995	66,990

RÖNISCH

Verticals

Model	Feet	Inches	Description	MSRP	SMP
118 K		46.5	Polished Ebony	23,367	23,367
118 K		46.5	Satin Mahogany	24,305	24,305
118 K		46.5	Polished Mahogany	28,356	28,356
118 K		46.5	Satin Walnut	24,518	24,305
118 K		46.5	Polished Walnut	28,569	28,569
118 K		46.5	Satin European Cherry	24,944	24,944
118 K		46.5	Satin German Oak	24,092	23,722
118 K		46.5	Polished White	25,499	25,499
118 K		46.5	Waxed Alder	23,239	23,239
118 K		46.5	Satin Heart Beech	23,665	23,665
118 K		46.5	Satin Ash	23,878	23,722
118 K		46.5	Satin Swiss Pear/Indian Apple	25,584	25,584
118 KI		46.5	Polished Mahogany w/Vavona Inlays	29,635	29,635
118 KI		46.5	Polished Walnut w/Burled Walnut Inlays	29,848	29,848
118 KI		46.5	Polished European Cherry w/Yew Inlays	30,274	30,274
118 KR		46.5	Polished Ebony	23,793	23,793

RÖNISCH *(continued)*

Model	Feet	Inches	Description	MSRP	SMP
118 KR		46.5	Polished White	25,925	25,925
118 M		46.5	Continental Polished Ebony	24,518	24,518
118 M		46.5	Continental Polished White	26,650	26,650
125 K		49	Polished Ebony	25,712	25,712
125 K		49	Satin Mahogany	26,138	26,138
125 K		49	Polished Mahogany	30,402	30,402
125 K		49	Satin Walnut	26,352	26,352
125 K		49	Polished Walnut	30,616	30,616
125 K		49	Satin European Cherry	26,778	26,746
125 K		49	Polished White	27,844	27,844
125 K		49	Carl Ronisch Edition Polished Burl Walnut	35,093	35,093
125 KI		49	Polished Mahogany w/Vavona Inlays	31,682	31,682
125 KI		49	Polished Walnut w/Burled Walnut Inlays	32,321	32,321
125 KI		49	Polished European Cherry w/Yew Inlays	32,321	32,321
125 KM		49	Polished Ebony	26,565	26,565
125 KM		49	Polished White	28,697	28,697
125 KN		49	Polished Ebony	27,418	27,418
125 KN		49	Polished White	29,550	29,550
125 KR		49	Polished Ebony	25,286	26,286
125 KR		49	Polished White	27,418	27,418
132 K		52	Polished Ebony	28,782	28,782
132 K		52	Satin Mahogany	29,208	29,208
132 K		52	Polished Mahogany	33,472	33,472
132 K		52	Satin Walnut	29,422	29,422
132 K		52	Polished Walnut	33,686	33,634
132 K		52	Polished White	30,914	30,914
132 K		52	Polished Bubinga	34,325	34,325
132 K		52	Carl Ronisch Edition Polished Burl Walnut	38,589	38,589
132 KM		52	Polished Ebony	29,635	29,635
132 KM		52	Polished White	31,767	31,767

Grands

Model	Feet	Inches	Description	MSRP	SMP
175 K	5	9	Polished Ebony	77,178	69,894
175 K	5	9	Satin Mahogany	78,884	71,452
175 K	5	9	Polished Mahogany	90,823	82,434
175 K	5	9	Satin Walnut	80,163	71,452
175 K	5	9	Polished Walnut	92,102	82,434
175 K	5	9	Satin European Cherry	82,295	74,568
175 K	5	9	Polished White	81,442	73,808
175 K	5	9	Polished Bubinga	95,514	86,728
175 K	5	9	Carl Ronisch Edition Polished Burl Walnut	107,026	97,292
175 KI	5	9	Polished Mahogany w/Vavona Inlays	110,011	100,066
175 KI	5	9	Polished Walnut w/Burled Walnut Inlays	112,143	102,004
175 KI	5	9	Polished European Cherry w/Yew Inlays	115,128	104,740
186 K	6	1	Polished Ebony	83,574	75,746
186 K	6	1	Satin Mahogany	85,280	78,520

Model	Feet	Inches	Description	MSRP	SMP
RÖNISCH *(continued)*					
186 K	6	1	Polished Mahogany	97,219	89,502
186 K	6	1	Satin Walnut	86,559	78,520
186 K	6	1	Polished Walnut	98,498	89,502
186 K	6	1	Satin European Cherry	88,691	80,458
186 K	6	1	Polished White	87,838	79,660
186 K	6	1	Polished Bubinga	101,910	92,618
186 K	6	1	Carl Ronisch Edition Polished Burl Walnut	113,422	103,182
186 KI	6	1	Polished Mahogany w/Vavona Inlays	116,407	105,956
186 KI	6	1	Polished Walnut w/Burled Walnut Inlays	118,539	108,274
186 KI	6	1	Polished European Cherry w/Yew Inlays	121,524	111,390
210 K	6	10.5	Polished Ebony	107,026	87,156
210 K	6	10.5	Polished White	111,290	90,658

SAMICK

Grands

Model	Feet	Inches	Description	MSRP	SMP
NSG 158	5	2	Satin Ebony	25,495	19,198
NSG 158	5	2	Polished Ebony	23,995	18,198
NSG 175	5	7	Satin Ebony	27,995	20,998
NSG 175	5	7	Polished Ebony	26,495	19,998
NSG 186	6	1	Satin Ebony	30,795	22,998
NSG 186	6	1	Polished Ebony	29,395	21,998
Grands			Other wood finishes, add	2,000	2,000

SAUTER

Standard wood veneers are walnut, mahogany, ash, and alder.

Verticals

Model	Feet	Inches	Description	MSRP	SMP
119		46	Peter Maly Concent Satin Ebony	32,000	32,000
119		46	Peter Maly Concent Polished Ebony	34,000	34,000
122		48	Ragazza Polished Ebony	36,500	36,500
122		48	Ragazza Satin Cherry	36,500	36,500
122		48	Ragazza Polished Cherry/Yew	43,000	43,000
122		48	Vista Polished Ebony	40,000	40,000
122		48	Vista Satin Maple	38,500	38,500
122		48	Vista Satin Cherry	40,000	40,000
122		48	Master Class Polished Ebony	47,000	47,000
122		48	Peter Maly Artes Polished Ebony	52,000	52,000
122		48	Peter Maly Artes Polished Palisander/Macassar	53,500	53,500
122		48	Peter Maly Artes Polished White	53,500	53,500
122		48	Peter Maly Pure Noble Polished Ebony/Veneers	49,000	49,000
122		48	Peter Maly Pure Noble Polished White/Red	50,000	50,000
122		48	Peter Maly Pure Basic Satin Ebony/Walnut	39,900	39,900
122		48	Peter Maly Pure Basic Satin White	39,900	39,900
122		48	Peter Maly Pure Basic Satin White/Maple	39,900	39,900

Model	Feet	Inches	Description	MSRP	SMP

SAUTER (continued)

Model	Feet	Inches	Description	MSRP	SMP
122		48	Peter Maly Rondo Polished Ebony	43,500	43,500
122		48	Peter Maly Rondo Satin Wenge	40,500	40,500
122		48	Peter Maly Vitrea Colored Ebony with Glass	41,000	41,000
122		48	Schulpiano Satin Beech/Black Ash	32,000	32,000
130		51	Master Class Polished Ebony	53,000	53,000
130		51	Competence Polished Ebony	45,500	45,500
130		51	Competence Satin Walnut	43,000	43,000
130		51	Sonder Polished Ebony w/Sostenuto	39,900	39,900
130		51	Sonder Polished Ebony w/o Sostenuto	36,000	36,000

Grands

Model	Feet	Inches	Description	MSRP	SMP
160	5	3	Alpha Polished Ebony	95,000	95,000
160	5	3	Alpha Satin Standard Wood Veneers	88,000	88,000
160	5	3	Chippendale Satin Cherry	99,000	99,000
160	5	3	Chippendale Satin Standard Wood Veneers	96,000	96,000
160	5	3	Noblesse Satin Cherry	106,000	106,000
160	5	3	Noblesse Polished Cherry	115,000	115,000
160	5	3	Noblesse Satin Burl Walnut	111,000	111,000
160	5	3	Noblesse Satin Standard Wood Veneers	106,000	106,000
160	5	3	Noblesse Polished Standard Wood Veneers	114,000	114,000
185	6	1	Delta Polished Ebony	106,000	106,000
185	6	1	Delta Polished Ebony w/Burl Walnut	110,000	110,000
185	6	1	Delta Polished Pyramid Mahogany	117,000	117,000
185	6	1	Delta Polished Bubinga	116,000	116,000
185	6	1	Delta Polished Rio Palisander	117,000	117,000
185	6	1	Delta Satin Maple with Silver	99,000	99,000
185	6	1	Delta Polished White	110,000	110,000
185	6	1	Delta Satin Standard Wood Veneers	98,000	98,000
185	6	1	Chippendale Satin Cherry	109,000	109,000
185	6	1	Chippendale Satin Standard Wood Veneers	105,000	105,000
185	6	1	Noblesse Satin Cherry	116,000	116,000
185	6	1	Noblesse Polished Cherry	129,000	129,000
185	6	1	Noblesse Satin Burl Walnut	121,000	121,000
185	6	1	Noblesse Satin Standard Wood Veneers	112,000	112,000
185	6	1	Noblesse Polished Standard Wood Veneers	126,000	126,000
210	6	11	Peter Maly Vivace Polished Ebony	150,000	150,000
210	6	11	Peter Maly Vivace Satin Wood Veneers	140,000	140,000
210	6	11	Peter Maly Vivace Polished White	150,000	150,000
220	7	3	Omega Polished Ebony	135,000	135,000
220	7	3	Omega Polished Burl Walnut	149,000	149,000
220	7	3	Omega Polished Pyramid Mahogany	148,000	148,000
220	7	3	Omega Satin Standard Wood Veneers	129,000	129,000
230	7	7	Peter Maly Ambiente Polished Ebony	170,000	170,000
230	7	7	Peter Maly Ambiente Polished Ebony w/Crystals	195,000	195,000
275	9		Concert Polished Ebony	230,000	230,000

PIANOBUYER *Model & Price Supplement*

Model	Feet	Inches	Description	MSRP	SMP
SCHIMMEL					
Classic Series Verticals					
C 116		46	Tradition Polished Ebony	24,915	20,932
C 116		46	Tradition Polished Mahogany/White	28,083	23,466
C 116		46	Tradition Satin Walnut/Cherry/Beech/Alder	24,915	20,932
C 116		46	Modern Polished Ebony	28,875	24,100
C 116		46	Modern Polished White	32,043	26,634
C 116		46	Modern Cubus Polished Ebony	28,875	24,100
C 116		46	Modern Cubus Polished White	32,043	26,634
C 120		48	Tradition Polished Ebony	27,028	22,622
C 120		48	Tradition Polished Mahogany/White	30,195	25,156
C 120		48	Tradition Satin Walnut/Cherry/Beech/Alder	27,028	22,622
C 120		48	Tradition Marketerie Polished Mahogany w/Inlay	32,305	26,844
C 120		48	Elegance Manhattan Polished Ebony	26,105	21,884
C 120		48	Elegance Manhattan Polished Mahogany/White	29,273	24,418
C 120		48	Royal Polished Ebony	29,665	24,732
C 120		48	Royal Intarsie Flora Polished Mahogany w/Inlays	34,945	28,956
C 126		50	Tradition Polished Ebony	32,833	27,266
C 126		50	Tradition Polished Mahogany/White	36,000	29,800
C 130		51	Tradition Polished Ebony	35,473	29,378
C 130		51	Tradition Polished Mahogany/White	38,640	31,912
Konzert Series Verticals					
K 122		48	Elegance Polished Ebony	36,398	30,118
K 125		49	Tradition Polished Ebony	39,038	32,230
K 125		49	Tradition Polished Mahogany	43,260	35,608
K 132		52	Tradition Polished Ebony	44,580	36,664
K 132		52	Tradition Polished Mahogany	48,803	40,042
Fridolin Schimmel Verticals					
F 116		46	Polished Ebony	7,838	7,270
F 116		46	Polished White	8,213	7,570
F 121		48	Polished Ebony	8,963	8,170
F 121		48	Polished Walnut/White	9,338	8,470
F 123		49	Polished Ebony	10,088	9,070
F 123		49	Polished Mahogany/White	10,463	9,370
Wilhelm Schimmel Verticals					
W 114		46	Tradition Polished Ebony	17,130	14,704
W 114		46	Tradition Polished Mahogany/White	19,770	16,816
W 114		46	Modern Polished Ebony	18,050	15,440
W 114		46	Modern Polished White	20,075	17,060
W 114		46	Modern Swing Polished Ebony	17,130	14,704
W 114		46	Modern Swing Polished Mahogany/White	19,770	16,816
W 118		48	Tradition Polished Ebony	18,715	15,972
W 118		48	Tradition Polished Mahogany/White	21,353	18,082
W 123		49	Tradition Polished Ebony	20,298	17,238
W 123		49	Tradition Polished Mahogany/White	22,938	19,350

Model	Feet	Inches	Description	MSRP	SMP

SCHIMMEL *(continued)*
Classic Series Grands

Model	Feet	Inches	Description	MSRP	SMP
C 169	5	7	Tradition Polished Ebony	67,938	55,350
C 169	5	7	Tradition Polished Mahogany/White	74,535	60,628
C 189	6	2	Tradition Polished Ebony	71,895	58,516
C 189	6	2	Tradition Polished Mahogany/White	78,495	63,796
C 213	7		Tradition Polished Ebony	78,495	63,796
C 213	7		Tradition Polished Mahogany/White	85,093	69,074

Konzert Series Grands

Model	Feet	Inches	Description	MSRP	SMP
K 175	5	9	Tradition Polished Ebony	86,870	70,496
K 175	5	9	Tradition Polished Mahogany/White	94,558	76,646
K 195	6	4	Tradition Polished Ebony	94,558	76,646
K 195	6	4	Tradition Polished Mahogany/White	102,245	82,796
K 213	7		Glas Clear Acrylic and White or Black and Gold	320,313	257,250
K 213	7		Otmar Alt Polished Ebony w/Color Motifs	230,625	185,500
K 219	7	2	Tradition Polished Ebony	102,245	82,796
K 219	7	2	Tradition Polished Mahogany/White	109,933	88,946
K 230	7	6	Tradition Polished Ebony	117,620	95,096
K 256	8	4	Tradition Polished Ebony	132,995	107,396
K 280	9	2	Tradition Polished Ebony	153,495	123,796

Wilhelm Schimmel Grands

Model	Feet	Inches	Description	MSRP	SMP
W 180	6		Tradition Polished Ebony	41,413	34,130
W 180	6		Tradition Polished Mahogany/White	46,693	38,354
W 206	6	10	Tradition Polished Ebony	50,650	41,520
W 206	6	10	Tradition Polished Mahogany/White	55,930	45,744

SCHULZ, GEBR.
Verticals

Model	Feet	Inches	Description	MSRP	SMP
G-20		48	Polished Ebony	9,995	9,590
G-20		48	Hand-rubbed Satin Walnut	12,895	12,500

Grands

Model	Feet	Inches	Description	MSRP	SMP
G-58	5	5	Polished Ebony	18,995	18,995
G-86	6		Polished Ebony	23,995	23,995
G-288	9		Polished Ebony	49,995	49,995

SCHULZE POLLMANN
Studio Series Verticals

Model	Feet	Inches	Description	MSRP	SMP
SU118A		46	Polished Peacock Ebony	15,995	8,990
SU118A		46	Polished Peacock Mahogany/Walnut	16,995	9,590
SU122A		48	Polished Peacock Ebony	18,995	10,390
SU122A		48	Polished Peacock Mahogany/Walnut	19,995	10,990

Model	Feet	Inches	Description	MSRP	SMP
SCHULZE POLLMANN *(continued)*					
SU122A		48	Polished Feather Mahogany	20,995	11,590
SU132A		52	Polished Peacock Ebony	23,995	12,990
Academy Series Verticals					
A-125E		50	Polished Ebony	26,995	14,390
A-125E		50	Polished Peacock Ebony	27,995	14,990
A-125E		50	Polished Peacock Mahogany/Walnut	30,995	16,590
A-125E		50	Polished Feather Mahogany	33,995	16,990
Masterpiece Series Grands					
160/GK	5	3	Polished Ebony (spade leg)	55,995	55,995
160/GK	5	3	Polished Briar Mahogany (spade leg)	59,995	59,995
160/GK	5	3	Polished Feather Mahogany (spade leg)	63,995	63,995
197/G5	6	6	Polished Ebony (spade leg)	77,995	76,990
197/G5	6	6	Polished Briar Mahogany (spade leg)	80,995	80,995
197/G5	6	6	Polished Feather Mahogany (spade leg)	84,995	84,995

SCHUMANN

Model	Feet	Inches	Description	MSRP	SMP
Verticals					
C1-112		44	Polished Ebony	5,995	4,990
C1-112		44	Polished Mahogany	6,195	5,390
K1-122		48	Polished Ebony	6,495	5,590
K1-122		48	Polished Mahogany	6,695	5,990
K1-122		48	Polished Walnut/White	6,695	6,190
K1-122		48	Polished White	6,695	6,190
Grands					
GP-152	5		Polished Ebony	11,900	9,590
GP-152	5		Polished White	12,900	10,090
GP-168	5	6	Polished Ebony	14,900	11,990
GP-168	5	6	Polished White	15,900	12,590
GP-186	6	2	Polished Ebony	18,995	13,190

SEILER

Model	Feet	Inches	Description	MSRP	SMP
Seiler Verticals					
SE-116		45	Primus, Polished Ebony	28,895	22,398
SE-116		45	Mondial, Polished Ebony	30,495	23,598
SE-116		45	Mondial, Polished Rosewood	41,295	31,598
SE-116		45	Konsole, Polished Ebony	34,595	26,598
SE-116		45	Impuls, Polished Ebony	30,495	23,598
SE-116		45	Clou, Polished Ebony	35,895	27,598
SE-116		45	Accent, Polished Ebony	35,895	27,598
SE-122		48	Primus, Polished Ebony	38,595	29,598

Model	Feet	Inches	Description	MSRP	SMP
SEILER (continued)					
SE-126		49	Konsole, Polished Ebony	42,695	32,598
SE-126		49	Konsole, Satin Walnut	43,995	33,598
SE-126		49	Attraction, Polished Ebony	45,695	34,798
SE-132		52	Consert, Polished Ebony	52,395	39,798
SE-132		52	Consert, Polished Ebony w/SMR	55,095	41,798
SE-132		52	Consert, Polished Ebony w/Rec Panel	55,095	41,798
SE-132		52	Consert, Polished Ebony w/Rec Panel/SMR	55,795	43,798
Eduard Seiler ED Series Verticals					
ED-126		49	Primus, Satin Ebony	13,295	10,798
ED-126		49	Primus, Polished Ebony	12,695	10,398
ED-126M		49	Primus, Satin Ebony w/SMR	14,595	11,798
ED-126M		49	Primus, Polished Ebony w/SMR	14,095	11,398
ED-132		52	Konzert, Satin Ebony	14,095	11,398
ED-132		52	Konzert, Polished Ebony	13,495	10,998
ED-132M		52	Konzert, Satin Ebony w/SMR	15,395	12,398
ED-132M		52	Konzert, Polished Ebony w/SMR	14,895	11,998
Verticals			Other wood finishes, add		1,500
Johannes Seiler Verticals					
GS-116N		45.5	Satin Ebony w/Nickel Hardware	9,999	8,398
GS-116N		45.5	Polished Ebony w/Nickel Hardware	9,395	7,998
GS-247		46.5	Satin Ebony	10,795	8,998
GS-247		46.5	Polished Ebony	9,995	8,398
GS-247		46.5	Satin Walnut	10,795	8,998
GS-118		47	Satin Ebony	10,195	8,598
GS-118		47	Polished Ebony	9,695	8,198
GS-121		47.5	Ditto, Polished Ebony w/Silver accent	11,595	9,598
GS-122		48.5	Satin Ebony	10,995	9,198
GS-122		48.5	Polished Ebony	10,195	8,598
Verticals			Other wood finishes, add		1,500
Seiler Grands					
SE-168	5	6	Virtuoso, Polished Ebony	96,395	72,398
SE-168	5	6	Virtuoso, Polished Mahogany	115,795	86,798
SE-186	6	2	Maestro, Polished Ebony	113,195	84,798
SE-186	6	2	Maestro, Polished Mahogany	121,295	90,798
SE-186	6	2	Maestro, Polished Rosewood	129,595	96,998
SE-186	6	2	Ziricote, Polished Ebony	122,595	91,798
SE-186	6	2	Louvre, Polished Cherry	152,895	114,198
SE-186	6	2	Florenz, Polished Mahogany	152,895	114,198
SE-208	6	10	Professional, Polished Ebony	126,895	94,998
SE-242	8		Konzert, Polished Ebony	167,895	125,398
SE-278	9	2	Konzert, Polished Ebony	272,695	202,998

Model	Feet	Inches	Description	MSRP	SMP

SEILER (continued)
Eduard Seiler ED Series Grands

Model	Feet	Inches	Description	MSRP	SMP
ED-168	5	6	Virtuoso, Satin Ebony	36,995	28,398
ED-168	5	6	Virtuoso, Polished Ebony	36,495	27,998
ED-168HS	5	6	Heritage, Satin Ebony	45,995	34,998
ED-168HS	5	6	Heritage, Polished Ebony	44,895	34,198
ED-186	6	2	Maestro, Satin Ebony	45,095	34,398
ED-186	6	2	Maestro, Polished Ebony	43,495	33,198
ED-186A	6	2	Custom, Polished Ebony	83,495	62,798
Grands			Other wood finishes, add		2,000

Johannes Seiler Grands

Model	Feet	Inches	Description	MSRP	SMP
GS-160	5	3	Satin Ebony	25,395	19,798
GS-160	5	3	Polished Ebony	23,995	18,798
GS-160LN	5	3	Satin Ebony (M Leg Style)	28,595	22,198
GS-160LN	5	3	Polished Ebony (M Leg Style)	27,295	21,198
GS-175	5	9	Satin Ebony	27,795	21,598
GS-175	5	9	Polished Ebony	26,395	20,598
GS-186	6	2	Satin Ebony	29,695	22,998
GS-186	6	2	Polished Ebony	28,595	22,198
Grands			Other wood finishes, add		2,000

STEINBERG, G.
Verticals

Model	Inches	Description	MSRP	SMP
RH-111 Nicosia	45	Polished Ebony	8,240	7,220
RH-111 Nicosia	45	Polished Mahogany/Walnut	8,460	7,430
RH-111 Nicosia	45	Polished White	8,680	7,640
RH-115 Slate	45	Polished Ebony	8,460	7,430
RH-115 Slate	45	Polished Mahogany/Walnut	8,680	7,550
RH-115 Slate	45	Polished White	9,010	7,780
RH-115 Slate	45	Queen Anne Polished Ebony	8,680	7,550
RH-115 Slate	45	Queen Anne Polished Mahogany/Walnut	8,900	7,660
RH-115 Slate	45	Queen Anne Polished White	9,120	7,880
RH-119 Splendit	47	Polished Ebony	8,900	7,860
RH-119 Splendit	47	Polished Mahogany/Walnut	9,120	8,070
RH-119 Splendit	47	Polished White	9,230	8,280
RH-119 Splendit	47	Queen Anne Polished Ebony	9,120	7,970
RH-119 Splendit	47	Queen Anne Polished Mahogany/Walnut	9,340	8,180
RH-119 Splendit	47	Queen Anne Polished White	9,450	8,380
RH-123 Performance	49	Polished Ebony	9,340	8,070
RH-123 Performance	49	Queen Anne Polished Ebony	9,670	8,280
RH-126 Sienna	50	Polished Ebony	10,440	8,700
RH-126 Sienna	50	Queen Anne Polished Ebony	10,770	8,900

Model	Feet	Inches	Description	MSRP	SMP

STEINBERG, G. *(continued)*
Grands

Model	Feet	Inches	Description	MSRP	SMP
GBT-152 Sovereign	5	1	Polished Ebony	19,470	14,710
GBT-152 Sovereign	5	1	Polished Mahogany/Walnut	21,200	15,820
GBT-152 Sovereign	5	1	Polished White	22,960	16,160
GBT-152 Sovereign	5	1	Queen Anne or Empire Polished Ebony	19,855	15,120
GBT-152 Sovereign	5	1	Queen Anne or Empire Polished Mahogany/Walnut	21,615	16,290
GBT-152 Sovereign	5	1	Queen Anne or Empire Polished White	23,485	16,560
GBT-160 Stockholm	5	5	Polished Ebony	25,160	16,910
GBT-160 Stockholm	5	5	Polished Mahogany/Walnut	26,975	17,950
GBT-160 Stockholm	5	5	Polished White	28,790	18,160
GBT-160 Stockholm	5	5	Queen Anne or Empire Polished Ebony	26,015	17,190
GBT-160 Stockholm	5	5	Queen Anne or Empire Polished Mahogany/Walnut	27,855	18,450
GBT-160 Stockholm	5	5	Queen Anne or Empire Polished White	29,670	18,660
GBT-175 Schwerin	5	10	Polished Ebony	28,460	17,620
GBT-175 Schwerin	5	10	Polished Mahogany/Walnut	29,725	19,080
GBT-175 Schwerin	5	10	Polished White	31,870	19,280
GBT-175 Schwerin	5	10	Queen Anne or Empire Polished Ebony	27,965	18,160
GBT-175 Schwerin	5	10	Queen Anne or Empire Polished Mahogany/Walnut	30,275	19,410
GBT-175 Schwerin	5	10	Queen Anne or Empire Polished White	33,190	19,620
GBT-187 Amsterdam	6	2	Polished Ebony	30,635	18,790
GBT-187 Amsterdam	6	2	Polished Mahogany/Walnut	31,870	19,820
GBT-187 Amsterdam	6	2	Polished White	34,155	20,030
GBT-187 Amsterdam	6	2	Queen Anne or Empire Polished Ebony	31,430	19,100
GBT-187 Amsterdam	6	2	Queen Anne or Empire Polished Mahogany/Walnut	32,475	20,240
GBT-187 Amsterdam	6	2	Queen Anne or Empire Polished White	34,510	20,450

STEINBERG, WILH.
Performance Series Verticals

Model	Inches	Description	MSRP	SMP
P118	45.5	Polished Ebony	8,280	6,590
P118	45.5	Polished White	9,390	7,290
P118C	45.5	Polished Ebony w/Chrome Hardware	8,490	6,690
P118C	45.5	Polished White w/Chrome Hardware	9,490	7,390
P121	47.5	Polished Ebony	9,490	7,390
P121	47.5	Polished White	10,490	8,090
P125E	49.5	Polished Ebony	10,990	8,590
P125EC	49.5	Polished Ebony w/Chrome Hardware	11,490	8,690

Signature Series Verticals

Model	Inches	Description	MSRP	SMP
S117	46	Polished Ebony	28,490	20,190
S117	46	Polished White	30,990	21,790

Model	Feet	Inches	Description	MSRP	SMP
STEINBERG, WILH. *(continued)*					
S117		46	Satin Mahogany/Walnut	31,490	21,990
S117		46	Polished Alder/Ash	32,190	22,490
S125		49	Polished Ebony	31,990	22,990
S125		49	Polished White	34,990	24,790
S125		49	Satin Mahogany/Walnut	35,990	24,990
S125		49	Polished Alder/Ash	34,990	25,690
S130		51	Polished Ebony	37,990	26,990
S130		51	Polished White	40,990	28,990
S130		51	Satin Mahogany/Walnut	42,190	29,190
S130		51	Polished Alder/Ash	43,590	30,090
Performance Series Grands					
P152	5		Polished Ebony	19,990	14,590
P152	5		Polished White	21,990	15,890
P165	5	5	Polished Ebony	23,490	16,990
P165	5	5	Polished White	25,490	18,290
P178	5	10	Polished Ebony	32,490	22,990
Signature Series Grands					
S188	6	2	Polished Ebony	79,990	54,980
S212	6	11	Polished Ebony	88,990	60,980

STEINGRAEBER & SÖHNE

Prices include bench.

Verticals

Model	Feet	Inches	Description	MSRP	SMP
122 T		48	Satin and Polished Ebony	47,950	46,700
122 T		48	Satin and Polished White	48,850	47,600
122 T		48	Polished Ebony w/Twist & Change Panels	54,000	52,750
122 T		48	Satin Ordinary Veneers	58,350	57,100
122 T		48	Polished Ordinary Veneers	64,060	62,810
122 T		48	Satin Special Veneers	60,300	59,050
122 T		48	Polished Special Veneers	66,030	64,780
122 T		48	Satin Extraordinary Veneers	73,070	71,820
122 T		48	Polished Extraordinary Veneers	78,800	77,550
122 T-SFM		48	Satin and Polished Ebony	50,660	49,410
122 T-SFM		48	Satin and Polished White	51,560	50,310
122 T-SFM		48	Polished Ebony w/Twist & Change Panels	56,670	55,420
122 T-SFM		48	Satin Ordinary Veneers	61,060	59,810
122 T-SFM		48	Polished Ordinary Veneers	66,750	65,500
122 T-SFM		48	Satin Special Veneers	62,990	61,740
122 T-SFM		48	Polished Special Veneers	68,700	67,450
122 T-SFM		48	Satin Extraordinary Veneers	75,780	74,530
122 T-SFM		48	Polished Extraordinary Veneers	81,530	80,280
130 T-PS		51	Satin and Polished Ebony	60,930	59,680
130 T-PS		51	Satin and Polished White	61,810	60,560

Model	Feet	Inches	Description	MSRP	SMP

STEINGRAEBER & SÖHNE *(continued)*

Model	Feet	Inches	Description	MSRP	SMP
130 T-PS		51	Polished Ebony w/Twist & Change Panels	66,960	65,710
130 T-PS		51	Satin Ordinary Veneers	71,300	70,050
130 T-PS		51	Polished Ordinary Veneers	77,020	75,770
130 T-PS		51	Satin Special Veneers	73,280	72,030
130 T-PS		51	Polished Special Veneers	78,990	77,740
130 T-PS		51	Satin Extraordinary Veneers	86,050	84,800
130 T-PS		51	Polished Extraordinary Veneers	91,760	90,510
130 T-SFM		51	Satin and Polished Ebony	62,110	60,860
130 T-SFM		51	Satin and Polished White	63,030	61,780
130 T-SFM		51	Polished Ebony w/Twist & Change Panels	68,130	66,880
130 T-SFM		51	Satin Ordinary Veneers	72,480	71,230
130 T-SFM		51	Polished Ordinary Veneers	78,190	76,940
130 T-SFM		51	Satin Special Veneers	74,430	73,180
130 T-SFM		51	Polished Special Veneers	80,140	78,890
130 T-SFM		51	Satin Extraordinary Veneers	87,240	85,990
130 T-SFM		51	Polished Extraordinary Veneers	92,950	91,700
138 K		54	Satin and Polished Ebony	64,580	63,330
138 K		54	Satin and Polished White	65,470	64,220
138 K		54	Polished Ebony w/Twist & Change Panels	70,590	69,340
138 K		54	Satin Ordinary Veneers	74,960	73,710
138 K		54	Polished Ordinary Veneers	80,650	79,400
138 K		54	Satin Special Veneers	76,890	75,640
138 K		54	Polished Special Veneers	82,620	81,370
138 K		54	Satin Extraordinary Veneers	89,720	88,470
138 K		54	Polished Extraordinary Veneers	95,430	94,180
138 K-SFM		54	Satin and Polished Ebony	67,250	66,000
138 K-SFM		54	Satin and Polished White	68,200	66,950
138 K-SFM		54	Polished Ebony w/Twist & Change Panels	73,300	72,050
138 K-SFM		54	Satin Ordinary Veneers	77,650	76,400
138 K-SFM		54	Polished Ordinary Veneers	83,360	82,110
138 K-SFM		54	Satin Special Veneers	79,620	78,370
138 K-SFM		54	Polished Special Veneers	85,350	84,100
138 K-SFM		54	Satin Extraordinary Veneers	92,390	91,140
138 K-SFM		54	Polished Extraordinary Veneers	98,120	96,870

Grands

Model	Feet	Inches	Description	MSRP	SMP
A-170	5	7	Satin and Polished Ebony	111,910	110,660
A-170	5	7	Satin and Polished White	114,390	113,140
A-170	5	7	Satin and Polished Ordinary Veneers	127,160	125,910
A-170	5	7	Satin and Polished Special Veneers	128,810	127,560
A-170	5	7	Satin and Polished Extraordinary Veneers	137,740	136,490
A-170 S	5	7	Studio Lacquer Anti-Scratch	106,110	104,860
B-192	6	3	Satin and Polished Ebony	129,360	128,110
B-192	6	3	Satin and Polished White	131,820	130,570
B-192	6	3	Satin and Polished Ordinary Veneers	146,310	145,060
B-192	6	3	Satin and Polished Special Veneers	148,180	146,930

Model	Feet	Inches	Description	MSRP	SMP
STEINGRAEBER & SÖHNE *(continued)*					
B-192	6	3	Satin and Polished Extraordinary Veneers	158,130	156,880
B-192 S	6	3	Studio Lacquer Anti-Scratch	123,310	122,060
C-212	7		Satin and Polished Ebony	147,400	146,150
C-212	7		Satin and Polished White	149,840	148,590
C-212	7		Satin and Polished Ordinary Veneers	165,500	164,250
C-212	7		Satin and Polished Special Veneers	167,580	166,330
C-212	7		Satin and Polished Extraordinary Veneers	178,630	177,380
C-212 S	7		Studio Lacquer Anti-Scratch	140,410	139,160
D-232	7	7	Satin and Polished Ebony	178,510	177,260
D-232	7	7	Satin and Polished White	180,970	179,720
D-232	7	7	Satin and Polished Ordinary Veneers	198,570	197,320
D-232	7	7	Satin and Polished Special Veneers	200,820	199,570
D-232	7	7	Satin and Polished Extraordinary Veneers	212,930	211,680
D-232 S	7	7	Studio Lacquer Anti-Scratch	170,030	168,780
E-272	8	11	Satin and Polished Ebony	258,250	257,000
E-272	8	11	Satin and Polished White	260,810	259,560
E-272	8	11	Satin and Polished Ordinary Veneers	282,480	281,230
E-272	8	11	Satin and Polished Special Veneers	284,370	283,120
E-272	8	11	Satin and Polished Extraordinary Veneers	300,150	298,900

STEINWAY & SONS

These are the prices at the Steinway retail store in New York City, often used as a benchmark for Steinway prices throughout the country. Model K-52 in ebony; model 1098 in ebony, mahogany, and walnut; and grand models in ebony, mahogany, and walnut include adjustable artist benches. Other models include regular wood bench. Wood-veneered models are in a semigloss finish called "satin lustre."

Verticals

Model	Feet	Inches	Description	MSRP	SMP
4510		45	Sheraton Satin Ebony	36,400	36,400
4510		45	Sheraton Mahogany	40,300	40,300
4510		45	Sheraton Walnut	40,800	40,800
1098		46.5	Satin Ebony	34,300	34,300
1098		46.5	Mahogany	38,100	38,100
1098		46.5	Walnut	38,600	38,600
K-52		52	Satin Ebony	40,000	40,000
K-52		52	Mahogany	45,000	45,000
K-52		52	Walnut	46,700	46,700

Grands

Model	Feet	Inches	Description	MSRP	SMP
S	5	1	Satin and Polished Ebony	71,800	71,800
S	5	1	Polished Ebony w/Sterling Hardware	73,800	73,800
S	5	1	Polished White	81,800	81,800
S	5	1	Mahogany	87,800	87,800
S	5	1	Walnut	88,800	88,800
S	5	1	Kewazinga Bubinga	93,800	93,800
S	5	1	East Indian Rosewood	108,800	108,800
S	5	1	Macassar Ebony	119,800	119,800

Model	Feet	Inches	Description	MSRP	SMP
STEINWAY & SONS *(continued)*					
S	5	1	Figured Sapele	93,800	93,800
S	5	1	Dark Cherry	93,800	93,800
S	5	1	Santos Rosewood	104,800	104,800
S	5	1	African Pommele	109,800	109,800
M	5	7	Satin and Polished Ebony	76,600	76,600
M	5	7	Polished Ebony w/Sterling Hardware	78,600	78,600
M	5	7	Polished White	86,600	86,600
M	5	7	Mahogany	92,600	92,600
M	5	7	Walnut	93,600	93,600
M	5	7	Kewazinga Bubinga	98,600	98,600
M	5	7	East Indian Rosewood	113,600	113,600
M	5	7	Macassar Ebony	124,600	124,600
M	5	7	Figured Sapele	98,600	98,600
M	5	7	Dark Cherry	98,600	98,600
M	5	7	Santos Rosewood	109,600	109,600
M	5	7	African Pommele	114,600	114,600
M 1014A	5	7	Chippendale Mahogany	107,600	107,600
M 1014A	5	7	Chippendale Walnut	108,600	108,600
M 501A	5	7	Louis XV Walnut	138,600	138,600
M 501A	5	7	Louis XV East Indian Rosewood	158,600	158,600
M Sketch 1111	5	7	The Teague Satin and Polished Ebony (Spirio only, included)	121,600	121,600
M Sketch 1111	5	7	The Teague Walnut (Spirio only, included)	131,600	131,600
M	5	7	Polished Ebony w/White/Color Pops Accessories	91,600	91,600
M	5	7	John Lennon Imagine Polished White	119,600	119,600
M	5	7	Onyx Duet Polished Ebony	113,600	113,600
M			Spirio Play (playback only) Player Piano System, add	25,000	25,000
O	5	10.5	Satin and Polished Ebony	85,800	85,800
O	5	10.5	Polished Ebony w/Sterling Hardware	87,800	87,800
O	5	10.5	Polished White	95,800	95,800
O	5	10.5	Mahogany	101,800	101,800
O	5	10.5	Walnut	102,800	102,800
O	5	10.5	Kewazinga Bubinga	107,800	107,800
O	5	10.5	East Indian Rosewood	122,800	122,800
O	5	10.5	Macassar Ebony	133,800	133,800
O	5	10.5	Figured Sapele	107,800	107,800
O	5	10.5	Dark Cherry	107,800	107,800
O	5	10.5	Santos Rosewood	118,800	118,800
O	5	10.5	African Pommele	123,800	123,800
O	5	10.5	Polished Ebony w/White/Color Pops Accessories	100,800	100,800
O	5	10.5	John Lennon Imagine Polished White	128,800	128,800
O	5	10.5	Onyx Duet Polished Ebony	122,800	122,800
A	6	2	Satin and Polished Ebony	99,100	99,100
A	6	2	Polished Ebony w/Sterling Hardware	101,100	101,100
A	6	2	Polished White	112,100	112,100

PIANOBUYER *Model & Price Supplement*

Model	Feet	Inches	Description	MSRP	SMP

STEINWAY & SONS *(continued)*

Model	Feet	Inches	Description	MSRP	SMP
A	6	2	Mahogany	118,100	118,100
A	6	2	Walnut	119,100	119,100
A	6	2	Kewazinga Bubinga	125,100	125,100
A	6	2	East Indian Rosewood	142,100	142,100
A	6	2	Macassar Ebony	155,100	155,100
A	6	2	Figured Sapele	123,100	123,100
A	6	2	Dark Cherry	124,100	124,100
A	6	2	Santos Rosewood	138,100	138,100
A	6	2	African Pommele	146,100	146,100
A	6	2	Polished Ebony w/White/Color Pops Accessories	116,100	116,100
A	6	2	John Lennon Imagine Polished White	151,100	151,100
A	6	2	Onyx Duet Polished Ebony	136,100	136,100
B	6	10.5	Satin and Polished Ebony	112,000	112,000
B	6	10.5	Polished Ebony w/Sterling Hardware	116,000	116,000
B	6	10.5	Polished White	125,000	125,000
B	6	10.5	Mahogany	131,000	131,000
B	6	10.5	Walnut	132,000	132,000
B	6	10.5	Kewazinga Bubinga	138,000	138,000
B	6	10.5	East Indian Rosewood	155,000	155,000
B	6	10.5	Macassar Ebony	168,000	168,000
B	6	10.5	Figured Sapele	136,000	136,000
B	6	10.5	Dark Cherry	137,000	137,000
B	6	10.5	Santos Rosewood	151,000	151,000
B	6	10.5	African Pommele	159,000	159,000
B	6	10.5	Polished Ebony w/White/Color Pops Accessories	129,000	129,000
B	6	10.5	John Lennon Imagine Polished White	164,000	164,000
B	6	10.5	Onyx Duet Polished Ebony	149,000	149,000
B			Spirio Play (playback only) Player Piano System, add	25,000	25,000
B			Spirio | r (playback and record) Player Piano System, add	40,000	40,000
D	8	11.75	Satin and Polished Ebony	176,300	176,300
D	8	11.75	Polished Ebony w/Sterling Hardware	180,300	180,300
D	8	11.75	Polished White	194,300	194,300
D	8	11.75	Mahogany	206,300	206,300
D	8	11.75	Walnut	207,300	207,300
D	8	11.75	Kewazinga Bubinga	217,300	217,300
D	8	11.75	East Indian Rosewood	247,300	247,300
D	8	11.75	Macassar Ebony	267,300	267,300
D	8	11.75	Figured Sapele	211,300	211,300
D	8	11.75	Dark Cherry	214,300	214,300
D	8	11.75	Santos Rosewood	233,300	233,300
D	8	11.75	African Pommele	258,300	258,300
D	8	11.75	Polished Ebony w/White/Color Pops Accessories	196,300	196,300
D	8	11.75	John Lennon Imagine Polished White	228,300	228,300
D	8	11.75	Spirio | r (playback and record) Player Piano System, add	40,000	40,000

Steinway (Hamburg) Grands

I frequently get requests for prices of pianos made in Steinway's branch factory in Hamburg, Germany. Officially, these pianos are not sold in North America, but it is possible to order one through an American Steinway dealer, or to go to Europe and purchase one there. The following list shows approximately how much it would cost to purchase a Hamburg Steinway in Europe and have it shipped to the United States. The list was derived by taking the published retail price in Europe, subtracting the value-added tax not applicable to foreign purchasers, converting to U.S. dollars (the rate used here is 1 Euro = $1.15, but is obviously subject to change), and adding approximate charges for duty, air freight, crating, insurance, brokerage fees, and delivery. Only prices for grands in polished ebony are shown here. Caution: This list is published for general informational purposes only. The price that Steinway would charge for a piano ordered through an American Steinway dealer may be different. (Also, the cost of a trip to Europe to purchase the piano is not included.)

Model	Feet	Inches	Description	MSRP	SMP
S-155	5	1	Polished Ebony	85,100	85,100
M-170	5	7	Polished Ebony	87,800	87,800
O-180	5	10.5	Polished Ebony	96,600	96,600
A-188	6	2	Polished Ebony	99,200	99,200
B-211	6	11	Polished Ebony	114,300	114,300
C-227	7	5.5	Polished Ebony	128,600	128,600
D-274	8	11.75	Polished Ebony	172,300	172,300

STORY & CLARK

All Story & Clark pianos include PNOscan, and USB and MIDI connectivity. In addition, all grands now include a QRS PNOmation player-piano system. Prices shown are those for online sales through www.qrsmusic.com.

Heritage Series Verticals

Model	Feet	Inches	Description	MSRP	SMP
H7		46	Academy Polished Ebony		5,395

Signature Series Verticals

Model	Feet	Inches	Description	MSRP	SMP
S8		48	Cosmopolitan Polished Ebony		5,395

Heritage Series Grands

Model	Feet	Inches	Description	MSRP	SMP
H50A	4	11	Prelude Polished Ebony/Mahogany		16,695
H60 QA	5		French Provincial Polished Ebony		17,495
H60 QA	5		French Provincial Satin Lacquer and Polished Mahogany		17,595
H60A	5	3	Academy Satin and Polished Ebony		17,495
H60A	5	3	Academy Polished Mahogany		17,495
H60A	5	3	Academy Polished White		17,995
H70A	5	7	Conservatory Polished Ebony		18,895
H80	6	1	Professional Polished Ebony		21,395
H90	6	10	Semi-Concert Polished Ebony		28,795

Signature Series Grands

Model	Feet	Inches	Description	MSRP	SMP
S500	4	11	Manhattan Semigloss Ebony w/Birdseye Maple Accents		25,095
S600	5	4	Cosmopolitan Polished Ebony		24,395
S600	5	4	Melrose Polished Ebony/Mahogany		26,995
S600	5	4	Park West Satin Ebony		24,195
S600	5	4	Park West Polished Ebony		24,495
S700	5	9	Fairfax Polished Ebony w/Bubinga Accents		26,695
S700	5	9	Versailles Satin Lacquer Cherry		26,295

Model	Feet	Inches	Description	MSRP	SMP

STORY & CLARK *(continued)*

Model	Feet	Inches	Description	MSRP	SMP
S700	5	9	Park West Polished Ebony		24,695
S800	6	2	Islander British Colonial Satin Walnut		27,895
S800	6	2	Park West Polished Ebony		25,395
S900	7		Park West Satin Ebony		38,495

WALTER, CHARLES R.

Verticals

Model	Feet	Inches	Description	MSRP	SMP
1520		43	Satin and Polished Walnut		18,477
1520		43	Satin and Polished Cherry		18,420
1520		43	Satin and Polished Oak		17,803
1520		43	Satin and Polished Mahogany		18,813
1520		43	Italian Provincial Satin and Polished Walnut		18,514
1520		43	Italian Provincial Satin and Polished Mahogany		18,850
1520		43	Italian Provincial Satin and Polished Oak		17,823
1520		43	Country Classic Satin and Polished Cherry		18,253
1520		43	Country Classic Satin and Polished Oak		17,923
1520		43	French Provincial Satin and Polished Oak		18,514
1520		43	French Provincial Satin and Polished Cherry/Walnut/Mahogany		19,072
1520		43	Riviera Satin and Polished Oak		17,752
1520		43	Queen Anne Satin and Polished Oak		18,666
1520		43	Queen Anne Satin and Polished Mahogany/Cherry		19,072
1500		45	Satin Ebony		17,172
1500		45	Semi-Gloss Ebony		17,506
1500		45	Polished Ebony (Lacquer)		17,707
1500		45	Polished Ebony (Polyester)		18,084
1500		45	Satin and Polished Oak		16,329
1500		45	Satin and Polished Walnut		17,358
1500		45	Satin and Polished Mahogany		17,619
1500		45	Satin and Polished Gothic Oak		17,380
1500		45	Satin and Polished Cherry		17,561
Verticals			Renner (German) action, add		1,925–2,150

Grands

Model	Feet	Inches	Description	MSRP	SMP
W-175	5	9	Satin Ebony		77,781
W-175	5	9	Semi-Polished and Polished Ebony (Lacquer)		79,776
W-175	5	9	Polished Ebony (Polyester)		80,863
W-175	5	9	Satin Mahogany/Walnut/Cherry		81,263
W-175	5	9	Semi-Polished & Polished Mahogany/Walnut/Cherry		83,334
W-175	5	9	Open-Pore Walnut		79,303
W-175	5	9	Satin Oak		74,766
W-175	5	9	Chippendale Satin Mahogany/Cherry		83,769
W-175	5	9	Chippendale Semi-Polished & Polished Mahogany/Cherry		85,804

Model	Feet	Inches	Description	MSRP	SMP

WALTER, CHARLES R. *(continued)*

Model	Feet	Inches	Description	MSRP	SMP
W-190	6	4	Satin Ebony		82,731
W-190	6	4	Semi-Polished and Polished Ebony (Lacquer)		84,817
W-190	6	4	Polished Ebony (Polyester)		85,947
W-190	6	4	Satin Mahogany/Walnut/Cherry		86,339
W-190	6	4	Semi-Polished & Polished Mahogany/Walnut/Cherry		88,485
W-190	6	4	Open-Pore Walnut		84,310
W-190	6	4	Satin Oak		79,598
W-190	6	4	Chippendale Satin Mahogany/Cherry		88,990
W-190	6	4	Chippendale Semi-Polished & Polished Mahogany/Cherry		91,051

WEBER

Weber Verticals

Model	Inches	Description	MSRP	SMP
W114	45	Polished Ebony	6,190	6,190
W114	45	Polished Mahogany	6,490	6,490
W121	48	Polished Ebony	6,990	6,980
W121	48	Polished Mahogany/Walnut/White	7,290	7,180
W131	52	Polished Ebony	7,690	7,380
W131	52	Polished Mahogany	7,990	7,780

Albert Weber Verticals

Model	Inches	Description	MSRP	SMP
AW 121	48	Polished Ebony	11,690	10,780
AW 121	48	Satin Mahogany	11,790	11,180
AW 121E	48	Polished Ebony w/Chrome	12,590	11,780
AW 131	52	Satin Ebony	14,000	13,780
AW 131	52	Polished Ebony	13,890	12,980

Weber Grands

Model	Feet	Inches	Description	MSRP	SMP
W150	4	11	Polished Ebony	13,990	12,780
W150	4	11	Polished Mahogany/Walnut/White	14,290	13,180
W150SP	4	11	Polished Ebony w/Chrome	14,690	13,580
W150SP	4	11	Polished White w/Chrome	14,790	13,780
W157	5	2	Polished Ebony	14,990	13,780
W157	5	2	Polished Mahogany	15,490	14,380
W175	5	9	Polished Ebony	16,990	15,580
W185	6	1	Polished Ebony	20,990	18,780

Albert Weber Grands

Model	Feet	Inches	Description	MSRP	SMP
AW 185	6	1	Polished Ebony	36,950	32,780
AW 208	6	10	Polished Ebony	45,550	39,780
AW 228	7	6	Polished Ebony	63,590	55,580
AW 275	9		Polished Ebony	115,190	98,580

Model	Feet	Inches	Description	MSRP	SMP

WERTHEIM

Verticals

Model	Feet	Inches	Description	MSRP	SMP
W121L		48	Polished Ebony	6,499	5,999
W123		48.5	Polished Ebony	6,999	6,499
W123		48.5	Polished Mahogany	7,299	6,999
WE123		48.5	Polished Ebony	8,999	8,499
WF125V1		49	Polished Ebony	17,999	16,999
WF125V3		49	Polished Ebony	11,999	11,299
W126		49.5	Polished Ebony	7,299	6,999

Grands

Model	Feet	Inches	Description	MSRP	SMP
W160	5	3	Polished Ebony	12,499	10,999
W160	5	3	Polished Mahogany	13,499	11,999
WF165	5	5	Polished Ebony	29,999	24,999
WE170	5	7	Polished Ebony	18,999	15,999
WE170	5	7	Polished Mahogany	19,999	14,999
WP180	5	11	Polished Ebony	29,999	24,999

YAMAHA
Including Disklavier, Silent, and TransAcoustic Pianos

Verticals

Model	Feet	Inches	Description	MSRP	SMP
b1		43	Continental Polished Ebony	4,799	4,799
b1		43	Continental Polished Ebony with Chrome Accents	4,999	4,999
b1		43	Continental Polished White	4,999	4,999
M560		44	Hancock Satin Brown Cherry	7,199	7,199
b2		45	Polished Ebony	6,749	6,598
b2		45	Polished Ebony with Chrome Accents	6,949	6,798
b2		45	Polished Mahogany/Walnut/White	7,159	6,998
P22		45	Satin Ebony/Walnut/Dark Oak	7,549	7,398
P660		45	Sheraton Satin Brown Mahogany	9,129	9,129
P660		45	Queen Anne Satin Brown Cherry	9,129	9,129
b3		48	Polished Ebony	8,259	7,798
b3		48	Polished Ebony with Chrome Accents	8,459	7,998
b3		48	Polished Mahogany/Walnut/White	9,129	8,298
U1		48	Satin and Polished Ebony	11,399	11,399
U1		48	Satin American Walnut	13,499	13,499
U1		48	Polished Mahogany/White	13,499	13,499
YUS1		48	Satin and Polished Ebony	15,599	14,998
YUS1		48	Satin American Walnut	18,799	17,930
YUS1		48	Polished Mahogany/White	18,799	17,930
U3		52	Polished Ebony	14,559	14,098
U3		52	Satin American Walnut	16,599	16,398
U3		52	Polished Mahogany	16,599	16,398
YUS3		52	Polished Ebony	18,899	17,998

Model	Feet	Inches	Description	MSRP	SMP
YAMAHA *(continued)*					
YUS3		52	Polished Mahogany	21,799	20,598
YUS5		52	Polished Ebony	20,999	19,978
SU7		52	Polished Ebony	39,999	38,390
Disklavier Verticals					
DU1ENST		48	Satin and Polished Ebony	29,099	27,558
DU1ENST		48	Satin American Walnut	31,199	29,698
DU1ENST		48	Polished Mahogany/White	31,199	29,698
DYUS1ENST		48	Satin and Polished Ebony	33,299	30,698
DYUS1ENST		48	Satin American Walnut	36,499	33,630
DYUS1ENST		48	Polished Mahogany/White	36,499	33,630
Silent and TransAcoustic Verticals					
b1SC2		43	Polished Ebony	9,299	9,398
b1SC2		43	Polished Ebony with Chrome Accents	9,499	9,698
b1SC2		43	Polished White	9,499	9,698
b2SC2		45	Polished Ebony	11,249	10,298
b2SC2		45	Polished Ebony with Chrome Accents	11,449	10,498
b2SC2		45	Polished Mahogany/Walnut/White	11,659	10,698
b3SC2		48	Polished Ebony	12,759	11,498
b3SC2		48	Polished Ebony with Chrome Accents	12,959	11,698
b3SC2		48	Polished Mahogany/Walnut/White	13,629	11,998
U1SH2		48	Satin and Polished Ebony	15,899	15,558
U1SH2		48	Satin American Walnut	17,999	17,698
U1SH2		48	Polished Mahogany/White	17,999	17,698
U1TA		48	Polished Ebony	17,399	17,058
YUS1SH2		48	Satin and Polished Ebony	20,099	18,698
YUS1SH2		48	Satin American Walnut	23,299	21,630
YUS1SH2		48	Polished Mahogany/White	23,299	21,630
YUS1TA		48	Polished Ebony	21,599	20,198
U3SH2		52	Polished Ebony	19,059	17,798
U3SH2		52	Polished Mahogany	21,099	20,098
U3SH2		52	Satin American Walnut	21,099	20,098
YUS3SH2		52	Polished Ebony	23,399	21,698
YUS3SH2		52	Polished Mahogany	26,299	24,298
YUS3TA		52	Polished Ebony	24,899	23,198
YUS5SH2		52	Polished Ebony	25,499	23,678
YUS5TA		52	Polished Ebony	26,999	25,178
Grands					
GB1K	5		Polished Ebony	14,999	14,158
GB1K	5		Polished American Walnut/Mahogany/White	17,339	16,198
GB1K	5		French Provincial Satin Cherry	19,179	18,598
GB1K	5		Georgian Satin Mahogany	18,359	18,198
GC1M	5	3	Satin and Polished Ebony	23,999	23,858
GC1M	5	3	Satin American Walnut	30,599	28,198

Model	Feet	Inches	Description	MSRP	SMP
YAMAHA (continued)					
GC1M	5	3	Polished Mahogany/White	30,599	28,198
C1X	5	3	Satin and Polished Ebony	37,999	34,098
C1X	5	3	Satin American Walnut	46,369	41,118
C1X	5	3	Polished Mahogany/White	46,369	41,118
GC2	5	8	Satin and Polished Ebony	28,959	26,998
GC2	5	8	Satin American Walnut	33,859	31,198
GC2	5	8	Polished Mahogany/White	33,859	31,198
C2X	5	8	Satin and Polished Ebony	43,999	40,198
C2X	5	8	Polished Ebony w/Chrome Accents	45,699	41,398
C2X	5	8	Satin American Walnut	53,399	47,938
C2X	5	8	Polished Mahogany/White	53,399	47,938
C3X	6	1	Satin and Polished Ebony	57,999	52,298
C3X	6	1	Satin American Walnut	69,999	62,798
C3X	6	1	Polished Mahogany/White	69,999	62,798
S3X	6	1	Polished Ebony	77,999	74,998
CF4	6	3	Polished Ebony	105,599	105,599
C5X	6	7	Satin and Polished Ebony	63,899	58,098
C5X	6	7	Satin American Walnut	77,799	69,560
C5X	6	7	Polished Mahogany/White	77,799	69,560
S5X	6	7	Polished Ebony	84,999	80,998
C6X	7		Satin and Polished Ebony	71,199	64,698
C6X	7		Satin American Walnut	85,999	77,718
C6X	7		Polished Mahogany/White	85,999	77,718
S6X	7		Polished Ebony	95,599	92,998
CF6	7		Polished Ebony	119,999	119,598
C7X	7	6	Satin and Polished Ebony	82,999	74,698
C7X	7	6	Satin American Walnut	99,999	89,478
C7X	7	6	Polished Mahogany/White	99,999	89,478
S7X	7	6	Polished Ebony	104,999	100,998
CFX	9		Polished Ebony	179,999	179,999
Disklavier Grands					
DGB1KENCL	5		Classic Polished Ebony (playback only)	23,999	23,158
DGB1KENST	5		Polished Ebony	28,599	26,758
DGB1KENST	5		Polished Mahogany/American Walnut/White	30,939	28,798
DGC1ENST	5	3	Satin and Polished Ebony	41,699	39,558
DGC1ENST	5	3	Satin American Walnut	48,299	43,898
DGC1ENST	5	3	Polished Mahogany/White	48,299	43,898
DC1XENST	5	3	Satin and Polished Ebony	55,699	49,798
DC1XENST	5	3	Satin American Walnut	64,069	56,818
DC1XENST	5	3	Polished Mahogany/White	64,069	56,818
DGC2ENST	5	8	Satin and Polished Ebony	46,659	42,698
DGC2ENST	5	8	Satin American Walnut	51,559	46,898
DGC2ENST	5	8	Polished Mahogany/White	51,559	46,898
DC2XENST	5	8	Satin and Polished Ebony	61,699	55,898

Model	Feet	Inches	Description	MSRP	SMP
YAMAHA (continued)					
DC2XENST	5	8	Polished Ebony w/Chrome Accents	63,399	57,098
DC2XENST	5	8	Satin American Walnut	71,099	63,638
DC2XENST	5	8	Polished Mahogany/White	71,099	63,638
DC3XENPRO	6	1	Satin and Polished Ebony	80,899	71,098
DC3XENPRO	6	1	Satin American Walnut	92,899	81,598
DC3XENPRO	6	1	Polished Mahogany/White	92,899	81,598
DS3XENPRO	6	1	Polished Ebony	117,999	112,998
DCF4ENPRO	6	3	Polished Ebony	145,599	144,198
DC5XENPRO	6	7	Satin and Polished Ebony	86,799	76,898
DC5XENPRO	6	7	Satin American Walnut	100,699	88,360
DC5XENPRO	6	7	Polished Mahogany/White	100,699	88,360
DS5XENPRO	6	7	Polished Ebony	124,999	118,998
DC6XENPRO	7		Satin and Polished Ebony	94,099	83,498
DC6XENPRO	7		Satin American Walnut	108,899	96,518
DC6XENPRO	7		Polished Mahogany/White	108,899	96,518
DS6XENPRO	7		Polished Ebony	135,599	130,998
DCF6ENPRO	7		Polished Ebony	159,999	157,598
DC7XENPRO	7	6	Satin and Polished Ebony	105,899	93,498
DC7XENPRO	7	6	Satin American Walnut	122,899	108,278
DC7XENPRO	7	6	Polished Mahogany/White	122,899	108,278
DS7XEMPRO	7	6	Polished Ebony	144,999	138,998
DCFXENPRO	9		Polished Ebony	219,999	218,998

Silent and TransAcoustic Grands

Model	Feet	Inches	Description	MSRP	SMP
GB1KSC2	5		Polished Ebony	19,499	17,858
GB1KSC2	5		Polished Mahogany/Walnut/White	21,839	19,898
GC1SH2	5	3	Satin and Polished Ebony	28,499	27,558
GC1SH2	5	3	Satin American Walnut	35,099	31,898
GC1SH2	5	3	Polished Mahogany/White	35,099	31,898
GC1TA	5	3	Polished Ebony	31,999	31,058
C1XSH2	5	3	Satin and Polished Ebony	42,499	37,798
C1XSH2	5	3	Satin American Walnut	50,869	44,818
C1XSH2	5	3	Polished Mahogany/White	50,869	44,818
C1XTA	5	3	Polished Ebony	45,499	41,298
GC2SH2	5	8	Satin and Polished Ebony	33,459	30,698
GC2SH2	5	8	Satin American Walnut	38,359	34,898
GC2SH2	5	8	Polished Mahogany/White	38,359	34,898
C2XSH2	5	8	Satin and Polished Ebony	48,499	43,898
C2XSH2	5	8	Polished Ebony w/Chrome Accents	50,199	45,098
C2XSH2	5	8	Satin American Walnut	57,899	51,638
C2XSH2	5	8	Polished Mahogany/White	57,899	51,638
C3XSH2	6	1	Satin and Polished Ebony	62,499	55,998
C3XSH2	6	1	Satin American Walnut	74,499	66,498
C3XSH2	6	1	Polished Mahogany/White	74,499	66,498

Model	Feet	Inches	Description	MSRP	SMP
YAMAHA *(continued)*					
C3XTA	6	1	Polished Ebony	65,999	59,498
C5XSH2	6	7	Satin and Polished Ebony	68,399	61,798
C5XSH2	6	7	Satin American Walnut	82,299	73,260
C5XSH2	6	7	Polished Mahogany/White	82,299	73,260
C6XSH2	7		Satin and Polished Ebony	75,699	68,398
C6XSH2	7		Satin American Walnut	90,499	81,418
C6XSH2	7		Polished Mahogany/White	90,499	81,418
C7XSH2	7	6	Satin and Polished Ebony	87,499	78,398
C7XSH2	7	6	Satin American Walnut	104,499	93,178
C7XSH2	7	6	Polished Mahogany/White	104,499	93,178

YOUNG CHANG

Verticals

Model	Feet	Inches	Description	MSRP	SMP
Y114		45	Polished Ebony	5,790	5,790
Y114		45	Polished Mahogany	6,250	6,250
Y114E		45	Polished Ebony w/Chrome	6,590	6,590
Y116		46	Polished Ebony	7,290	7,290
Y116		46	Satin Ebony/Walnut	7,390	7,390
Y121		48	Polished Ebony	6,890	6,800
Y121		48	Polished Mahogany/Walnut/White	6,890	6,890
Y131		52	Polished Ebony	7,390	7,300
Y131		52	Polished Mahogany	7,590	7,500

Grands

Model	Feet	Inches	Description	MSRP	SMP
Y150	4	11	Polished Ebony	12,990	12,180
Y150	4	11	Polished Mahogany/Walnut/White	13,490	12,580
Y150SP	4	11	Polished Ebony w/Chrome	13,790	12,780
Y157	5	2	Polished Ebony	13,990	12,980
Y157	5	2	Polished Mahogany	14,590	13,780
Y175	5	9	Polished Ebony	15,990	14,580
Y185	6	1	Polished Ebony	19,990	17,780

Digital Piano
Specifications & Prices

In the specification chart for each brand of digital piano, we have included those features and specifications about which buyers, in our experience, are most likely to be curious. However, many models have more features than are shown. See the various articles on digital pianos on our website for more information about each of the terms defined below, shown in the order in which they appear in the charts.

Form The physical form of the model: G=Grand, V= Vertical (Console), S=Slab.

Ensemble A digital piano with easy-play and auto-accompaniments (not just rhythms).

Finish The wood finishes or colors available for a particular model (not always specified for slab models). Multiple finish options are separated by a slash (/). A manufacturer's own color term is used where a generic term could not be determined. See the box below for finish codes.

FINISH CODES			
A	Ash	**O**	Oak
AG	Amber Glow	**Or**	Orange
Al	Alder	**P**	Polished (used with a wood or color designation)
Bl	Blue		
Bk	Black	**Pk**	Pink
C	Cherry	**R**	Rosewood
DB	Deep Brunette	**Rd**	Red
E	Ebony	**S**	Satin (used with a wood or color designation)
G	Gold		
Iv	Ivory	**Sr**	Silver
L	Lacquer (used with a wood or color designation)	**VR**	Velvette Rouge
		W	Walnut
M	Mahogany	**WG**	Wood Grain (wood type not specified)
MD	Mahogany Decor	**Wt**	White

Estimated Price This is our estimate of the price you will pay for the instrument. For digitals sold online or through chain and warehouse outlets, this price is the Minimum Advertised Price (MAP) and is shown in italics. For digitals sold only through bricks-and-mortar piano dealers, the price shown is based on a profit margin that piano dealers typically aspire to when selling digitals, including an allowance for incoming freight and setup. Discounts from this price, if any, typically are small. For more information on MAP and other pricing issues, please read "Buying a Digital Piano," elsewhere in this issue.

MSRP Manufacturer's Suggested Retail Price, also known as "list" or "sticker" price. Not all manufacturers use them.

Sound Source Indicates whether the sound source is Sampling (S) or Physical Modeling (M).

Voices The number of different musical voices the user can select from the instrument panel, plus (if applicable) the number of General MIDI (GM) or XG voices that are not user-selectable but are available for playback of MIDI files.

Key Off Indicates the presence of samples or simulation of Key Off sounds—acoustic piano keys and dampers returning to rest position and cutting off the sounds of vibrating strings.

Sustain Indicates the presence of samples or simulation of the sound with the sustain pedal depressed (allowing the strings to vibrate sympathetically).

String Resonance Indicates the presence of samples or simulation of String Resonance—the resonance sound of the strings of non-played notes.

Rhythms/Styles The number of rhythms in a standard digital, or the number of auto-accompaniment styles available in an ensemble digital.

Polyphony The maximum number of sounds the instrument can produce simultaneously. UL=Unlimited

Total Watts Total combined amplifier power.

Speakers The number of individual speakers.

Piano Pedals The number of piano pedals supplied with the model. A number in parentheses indicates the availability of an optional pedal unit with additional pedals.

Half Pedal Indicates that the model supports half-pedaling.

Action Indicates the type of action used, if specified.

Triple-Sensor Keys Indicates the presence of three key sensors, instead of the usual two, for greater touch realism.

Escapement Indicates the presence of an acoustic piano action's escapement feel.

Wood Keys Indicates actions with wooden keys.

Ivory Texture Indicates actions with ivory-textured keytops.

Bluetooth Indicates that the instrument is equipped with Bluetooth for connecting to theInternet.

Vocal Support The model supports some level of vocal performance. This support can vary from the piano simply having a microphone input, to its having the ability to produce the vocalist's voice in multi-part harmony, to pitch-correct the notes sung by the vocalist, or to alter the original voice.

Educational Features The model includes features that specifically support the learning experience. Note that while the ability to record and play back is an important learning tool, it is present on almost all models and so is not included in this definition.

External Storage Indicates the type of external memory storage accessible, such as USB or SanDisk.

USB to Computer Indicates the model's ability to interface with a Mac or PC via USB cable.

USB Digital Audio Indicates the ability to record and play back digital audio via a USB flash drive.

Recording Tracks The number of internal recordable tracks for recording of MIDI files.

Warranty (Parts/Labor) Indicates the manufacturer's warranty coverage period: the first number is the length of the parts coverage; the second number is the length of the labor coverage.

Dimensions Width, Depth, and Height are rounded to the nearest inch.

Weight Weight of the model rounded to the nearest pound.

Brand & Model	Form	Ensemble	Finish	Estimated Price	MSRP	Sound Source	Voices	Key Off	Sustain	String Resonance	Rhythms/Styles	Polyphony	Total Watts	Speakers	Piano Pedals	Half Pedal
Blüthner																
e-Klavier PRO-88 EX	S		ESL	2,736	3,326	S	35+ 256GM	Y	Y	Y		256	60	2	3 (5)	Y
e-Klavier 2	V		ESL/WtSL	5,704	6,381	S	35+ 256GM	Y	Y	Y		256	100	4	3	Y
e-Klavier 2	V		EPL	6,534	7,389	S	35+ 256GM	Y	Y	Y		256	100	4	3	Y
e-Klavier 3	V		ESL/WtSL	6,508	7,358	S	25+ 127GM	Y	Y	Y		256	150	4	3	Y
e-Klavier 3	V		EPL	7,337	8,366	S	25+ 127GM	Y	Y	Y		256	150	4	3	Y
e-Klavier Pianette	V		EPL	15,907	18,782	S	35+ 256GM	Y	Y	Y		256	150	4	3	Y
e-Klavier Homeline	V		ES	4,322	4,701	S	35+ 256GM	Y	Y	Y		256	60	4	3	Y
e-Klavier Homeline	V		Stained wood	4,599	5,037	S	35+ 256GM	Y	Y	Y		256	60	4	3	Y
e-Klavier Homeline	V		Waxed beechwood	4,875	5,373	S	35+ 256GM	Y	Y	Y		256	60	4	3	Y
e-Grand Studio	G		ESL/WtSL	11,279	12,936	S	35+ 256GM	Y	Y	Y		256	150	4	3	Y
e-Grand Studio	G		EPL/WtPL	13,767	15,960	S	35+ 256GM	Y	Y	Y		256	150	4	3	Y
e-Grand Concert	G		ESL/WtSL	15,978	18,648	S	35+ 256GM	Y	Y	Y		256	150	6	3	Y
e-Grand Concert	G		EPL/WtPL	19,261	22,638	S	35+ 256GM	Y	Y	Y		256	150	6	3	Y
Casio																
PX-5S	S		Wt	999	1,399	S	242+ 128GM	Y	Y	Y		256	0	0	1 (2)	
PX-160	S		Bk/G	499	799	S	18		Y			128	16	2	1 (3)	Y
PX-360	S	E	Bk	899	1,199	S	422+ 128GM	Y	Y	Y	200	128	16	4	1 (3)	Y
PX-560	S	E	Bl	1,199	1,599	S	522+ 128GM	Y	Y	Y	230	256	16	4	1 (3)	Y
PX-770	V		Bk/W/Wt	699	1,099	S	19		Y			128	16	2	3	Y
PX-780	V	E	Bk	899	1,399	S	122+ 128GM		Y	Y	180	128	40	4	3	Y
PX-870	V		Bk/W/Wt	999	1,499	S	19	Y	Y	Y		256	40	4	3	Y
PX-S1000	S		Bk/Wt	599	899	S	18	Y	Y	Y		192	16	2	1 (3)	Y
PX-S3000	S	E	Bk	799	1,099	S	572+ 128GM	Y	Y	Y	200	192	16	2	1 (3)	Y
CDP-S350	S	E	Bk	499	799	S	572+ 128GM		Y		200	64	16	2	1 (3)	Y
CGP-700	V	E	Bk	799	1,099	S	422+ 128GM		Y		200	128	40	6	1 (3)	Y
AP-270	V		Bk/W/Wt	1,049	1,499	S	22		Y			192	16	2	3	Y
AP-470	V		Bk/W/Wt	1,499	1,899	S	22	Y	Y	Y		256	40	4	3	Y

Brand & Model	Action	Triple-Sensor Keys	Escapement	Wood Keys	Ivory Texture	Bluetooth	Vocal Support	Educational Features	External Storage	USB to Computer	USB Digital Audio	Recording Tracks	Warranty (Parts/Labor)	Dimensions WxDxH (Inches)	Weight (Pounds)
Blüthner															
e-Klavier PRO-88 EX	4-zone graded				Y		Y		USB	Y	Y	1	2	55x17x5	30
e-Klavier 2	4-zone graded			Y	Y	Y			USB	Y	Y	1	2	55x25x42	220
e-Klavier 2	4-zone graded			Y	Y	Y			USB	Y	Y	1	2	55x25x42	220
e-Klavier 3	4-zone graded			Y	Y	Y			USB	Y	Y	1	2	55x25x42	230
e-Klavier 3	4-zone graded			Y	Y	Y			USB	Y	Y	1	2	55x25x42	230
e-Klavier Pianette	4-zone graded			Y	Y	Y			USB	Y	Y	1	2	55x25x42	220
e-Klavier Homeline	4-zone graded		Y				Y		USB	Y	Y	1	2	140x60x35	135
e-Klavier Homeline	4-zone graded		Y				Y		USB	Y	Y	1	2	140x60x35	135
e-Klavier Homeline	4-zone graded		Y				Y		USB	Y	Y	1	2	140x60x35	135
e-Grand Studio	4-zone graded			Y	Y	Y			USB	Y	Y	1	2	51x33x35	225
e-Grand Studio	4-zone graded			Y	Y	Y			USB	Y	Y	1	2	51x33x35	225
e-Grand Concert	4-zone graded			Y	Y	Y			USB	Y	Y	1	2	51x55x35	248
e-Grand Concert	4-zone graded			Y	Y	Y			USB	Y	Y	1	2	51x55x35	248
Casio															
PX-5S	Weighted, Scaled, Hammer Action	Y			Y				USB	Y	Y	8	3/3	52x11x5	24
PX-160	Weighted, Scaled, Hammer Action	Y			Y			Y		Y		2	3/3	52x12x6	26
PX-360	Weighted, Scaled, Hammer Action	Y			Y			Y	USB	Y	Y	17	3/3	52x12x6	26
PX-560	Weighted, Scaled, Hammer Action	Y			Y			Y	USB	Y	Y	17	3/3	52x12x6	27
PX-770	Weighted, Scaled, Hammer Action	Y			Y			Y		Y		12	3/3	55x12x31	69
PX-780	Weighted, Scaled, Hammer Action	Y			Y			Y	USB	Y	Y	17	3/3	53x12x33	70
PX-870	Weighted, Scaled, Hammer Action	Y			Y			Y	USB	Y	Y	2	3/3	55x12x30	76
PX-S1000	Weighted, Scaled, Hammer Action				Y	Y		Y	USB	Y		2	3/3	52x9x4	25
PX-S3000	Weighted, Scaled, Hammer Action				Y	Y		Y	USB	Y	Y	3	3/3	52x9x4	25
CDP-S350	Weighted, Scaled, Hammer Action				Y			Y	USB	Y		6	3/3	52x9x4	24
CGP-700	Weighted, Scaled, Hammer Action	Y			Y			Y	USB	Y	Y	16	3/3	52x12x31	57
AP-270	Weighted, Scaled, Hammer Action	Y			Y			Y		Y		2	5/5	56x17x32	81
AP-470	Weighted, Scaled, Hammer Action	Y			Y			Y	USB	Y	Y	2	5/5	54x17x33	96

Digital Piano Specifications & Prices

Brand & Model	Form	Ensemble	Finish	Estimated Price	MSRP	Sound Source	Voices	Key Off	Sustain	String Resonance	Rhythms/Styles	Polyphony	Total Watts	Speakers	Piano Pedals	Half Pedal
Casio *(continued)*																
AP-650	V	E	Bk	1,899	2,299	S	122+128GM	Y	Y	Y	180	256	60	4	3	Y
AP-700	V		Bk	2,499	2,999	S	26	Y	Y	Y		256	60	6	3	Y
GP-300	V		Bk/Wt	3,636	3,999	S	26	Y	Y	Y		256	100	6	3	Y
GP-400	V		Bk	4,273	4,999	S	35	Y	Y	Y		256	100	6	3	Y
GP-500	V		BkP	4,909	5,999	S	35	Y	Y	Y		256	100	6	3	Y
Dexibel																
VIVO P7	S	E	Bk	1,899	2,199	M/S	79	Y	Y	Y		UL	70	2	0 (2)	Y
VIVO S7	S	E	Bk	1,999	2,299	M/S	79	Y	Y	Y		UL	0	0	0 (3)	Y
VIVO S7 PRO	S	E	Wt	2,499	2,799	M/S	113	Y	Y	Y		UL		0	1 (3)	Y
VIVO S9	S	E	Wt	3,999	4,499	M/S	185	Y	Y	Y		UL		0	1 (3)	Y
VIVO H1	S	E	Bk	1,999	2,499	M/S	79	Y	Y	Y		UL	70	2	3	Y
VIVO H3	V	E	Bk/Wt	2,499	2,999	M/S	79	Y	Y	Y		UL	70	4	3	Y
VIVO H3S	V	E	Pk/Bl	2,999	3,499	M/S	79	Y	Y	Y		UL	70	4	3	Y
VIVO H7	V	E	Bk/Wt/Rd	3,999	4,499	M/S	79	Y	Y	Y		UL	112	5	3	Y
VIVO H7	V	E	EP/WtP/RdP	4,499	4,999	M/S	79	Y	Y	Y		UL	112	5	3	Y
Dynatone																
SDP-600	V		EP	3,809	5,795	s	33+128GM		Y	Y		256	100	4	3	Y
SDP-600	V		WtP	3,991	6,095	s	33+128GM		Y	Y		256	100	4	3	Y
SLP-210	V		R	1,627	2,195	s	18+128GM					81	24	2	3	
SLP-250H	V		Bk	2,173	3,095	s	33+128GM		Y	Y		256	30	4	3	Y
DPR-3200H	V	E	Bk	2,900	4,195	s	138	Y	Y	Y	80	256	100	4	3	Y
DPR-3500	V	E	Bk	3,445	5,095	s	138	Y	Y	Y	80	256	100	6	3	Y
SGP-600	G		EP	5,173	7,695	s	33+128GM		Y	Y		256	100	4	3	Y
SGP-600	G		WtP	5,355	7,995	S	33+128GM		Y	Y		256	100	4	3	Y
GPR-3500	G	E	EP	5,900	8,895	S	138	Y	Y	Y	80	256	100	6	3	Y
GPR-3500	G	E	WtP	6,082	9,195	S	138	Y	Y	Y	80	256	100	6	3	Y
VGP-4000Q	G	E	EP	9,173	14,495	S	138	Y	Y	Y	80	256	100	6	3	Y
VGP-4000Q	G	E	WtP	9,355	14,795	S	138	Y	Y	Y	80	256	100	6	3	Y

Brand & Model	Action	Triple-Sensor Keys	Escapement	Wood Keys	Ivory Texture	Bluetooth	Vocal Support	Educational Features	External Storage	USB to Computer	USB Digital Audio	Recording Tracks	Warranty (Parts/Labor)	Dimensions WxDxH (Inches)	Weight (Pounds)
Casio (continued)															
AP-650	Weighted, Scaled, Hammer Action	Y			Y			Y	USB	Y	Y	17	5/5	54x17x36	111
AP-700	Weighted, Scaled, Hammer Action	Y			Y			Y	USB	Y	Y	2	5/5	54x17x36	106
GP-300	Weighted, Scaled, Hammer Action	Y	Y	Y				Y	USB	Y	Y	2	5/5	57x19x38	171
GP-400	Weighted, Scaled, Hammer Action	Y	Y	Y				Y	USB	Y	Y	2	5/5	58x19x39	189
GP-500	Weighted, Scaled, Hammer Action	Y	Y	Y				Y	USB	Y	Y	2	5/5	57x19x38	171
Dexibel															
VIVO P7	Weighted	Y			Y		Y	Y	USB	Y	Y		3	52x15x5	32
VIVO S7	Weighted	Y		Y	Y		Y		USB	Y	Y		3	52x15x5	39
VIVO S7 PRO	Progressive Hammer	Y		Y	Y		Y	Y	USB	Y	Y		3	50x14x5	40
VIVO S9	Progressive Hammer	Y	Y	Y	Y		Y		USB	Y	Y		3	59x21x9	49
VIVO H1	Weighted	Y					Y	Y	USB	Y	Y		5	56x14x31	99
VIVO H3	Weighted	Y						Y	USB	Y	Y		5	56x14x31	97
VIVO H3S	Weighted	Y					Y	Y	USB	Y	Y		5	56x14x31	97
VIVO H7	Weighted, graded	Y		Y	Y		Y		USB	Y	Y		5	56x14x31	137
VIVO H7	Weighted, graded	Y		Y	Y		Y		USB	Y	Y		5	56x14x31	137
Dynatone															
SDP-600	New RHA-3W	Y	Y					Y		Y	Y	1	3/3	55x16x39	218
SDP-600	New RHA-3W	Y	Y					Y		Y	Y	1	3/3	55x16x39	218
SLP-210	New RHA							Y		Y	Y	2	3/3	54x16x33	75
SLP-250H	ARHA-I				Y			Y		Y	Y	1	3/3	54x16x33	95
DPR-3200H	ARHA-3I	Y			Y			Y	USB	Y	Y	2	3/3	55x19x35	127
DPR-3500	New RHA-3W	Y	Y			Y	Y		USB	Y	Y	2	3/3	55x19x35	119
SGP-600	New RHA-3W	Y		Y				Y		Y	Y	1	3/3	55x36x31	176
SGP-600	New RHA-3W	Y		Y				Y		Y	Y	1	3/3	55x36x31	176
GPR-3500	New RHA-3W	Y		Y			Y	Y	USB	Y	Y	2	3/3	56x46x36	209
GPR-3500	New RHA-3W	Y		Y			Y	Y	USB	Y	Y	2	3/3	56x46x36	209
VGP-4000Q	New RHA-3W	Y		Y			Y	Y	USB	Y	Y	2	3/3	60x56x40	440
VGP-4000Q	New RHA-3W	Y		Y			Y	Y	USB	Y	Y	2	3/3	60x56x40	440

Brand & Model	Form	Ensemble	Finish	Estimated Price	MSRP	Sound Source	Voices	Key Off	Sustain	String Resonance	Rhythms/Styles	Polyphony	Total Watts	Speakers	Piano Pedals	Half Pedal
Galileo																
YP200	V		R	2,495	3,495	S	19		Y	Y			128	80	4	3	
YP300	V		R	2,995	3,995	S	20		Y	Y			128	100	4	3	
YP300	V		EP	3,495	4,495	S	20		Y	Y			128	100	4	3	
Milano 3	V	E	R	4,995	5,995	S	138					100	64	40	4	3	
GYP300	G		EP/MP/WtP	6,995	8,995	S	20		Y	Y			128	120	4	3	
Milano 3G	G	E	EP	5,995	7,995	S	138					100	64	120	4	3	
Kawai																
ES110	S		Bk/Wt	699	1,049	S	19	Y	Y	Y		100	192	14	2	1 (3)	Y
MP7SE	S		Bk	1,799	2,199	S	256	Y	Y	Y		100	256	0	0	1 (3)	Y
MP11SE	S		Bk	2,799	3,299	S	40	Y	Y	Y		100	256	0	0	3	Y
VPC1	S		Bk	1,849	2,149		0							0	0	3	Y
ES8	S		Bk/Wt	1,649	2,499	S	34	Y	Y	Y		100	256	30	2	1 (3)	Y
CL26	V		R	1,099	1,495	S	8		Y				96	30	2	1	Y
CE220	V		ES	1,899	2,199	S	22		Y	Y		100	192	40	2	3	Y
KDP70	V		R	899	1,099	S	15	Y		Y			192	16	2	3	Y
KDP110	V		R	1,149	1,499	S	15	Y		Y			192	40	2	3	Y
CN27	V		R	1,899	2,299	S	19	Y	Y	Y			192	40	2	3	Y
CN37	V		R	2,599	3,199	S	352	Y	Y	Y		100	256	40	4	3	Y
CN37	V		WtS/ES	2,699	3,299	S	352	Y	Y	Y		100	256	40	4	3	Y
CA48	V		R	2,099	2,499	S	19	Y	Y	Y		100	192	40	4	3	Y
CA48	V		ES	2,199	2,499	S	19	Y	Y	Y		100	192	40	4	3	Y
CA58	V		R	2,999	3,949	S	42	Y	Y	Y		100	256	100	4	3	Y
CA58	V		WtS/ES	3,099	3,999	S	42	Y	Y	Y		100	256	100	4	3	Y
CA78	V		R	3,999	4,999	M/S	66	Y	Y	Y		100	256	100	6	3	Y
CA78	V		WtS/ES	4,099	5,099	M/S	66	Y	Y	Y		100	256	100	6	3	Y
CA78	V		EP	4,699	5,799	M/S	66	Y	Y	Y		100	256	100	6	3	Y
CA98	V		R	5,399	6,799	M/S	88	Y	Y	Y		100	256	135	6	3	Y
CA98	V		ES	5,499	6,799	M/S	88	Y	Y	Y		100	256	135	6	3	Y
CA98	V		EP	6,199	7,699	M/S	88	Y	Y	Y		100	256	135	6	3	Y

Brand & Model	Action	Triple-Sensor Keys	Escapement	Wood Keys	Ivory Texture	Bluetooth	Vocal Support	Educational Features	External Storage	USB to Computer	USB Digital Audio	Recording Tracks	Warranty (Parts/Labor)	Dimensions WxDxH (Inches)	Weight (Pounds)
Galileo															
YP200	Grand Response									Y		0	4/1	54x17x39	119
YP300	Graded Hammer									Y		3	4/1	54x20x41	137
YP300	Graded Hammer									Y		3	4/1	54x20x41	137
Milano 3	Graded Hammer									Y		3	4/1	56x20x34	154
GYP300	Graded Hammer									Y		3	4/1	56x29x35	209
Milano 3G	Graded Hammer									Y		3	4/1	56x29x35	200
Kawai															
ES110	RHC					Y	Y					1	3/3	52x11x6	26
MP7SE	RHIII	Y	Y		Y				USB	Y	Y	1	3/1	53x13x7	45
MP11SE	GF	Y	Y	Y	Y				USB	Y	Y	1	3/1	58x18x8	72
VPC1	RM3II	Y	Y	Y	Y					Y		0	3/1	54x18x8	65
ES8	RHIII	Y	Y		Y				USB	Y	Y	2	3/3	54x15x6	46
CL26	AHA IV-F											0	3/3	51x11x31	63
CE220	AWA PROII				Y				USB	Y		2	3/3	55x20x34	137
KDP70	RHC						Y			Y		1	3/3	54x16x34	77
KDP110	RHCII	Y				Y	Y			Y		1	3/3	54x16x34	86
CN27	RHIII	Y	Y			Y	Y	Y		Y		1	5/5	54x16x34	95
CN37	RHIII	Y	Y			Y	Y	Y	USB	Y	Y	2	5/5	57x18x34	122
CN37	RHIII	Y	Y			Y	Y	Y	USB	Y	Y	2	5/5	57x18x34	122
CA48	GFC	Y	Y	Y	Y	Y		Y		Y		1	5/5	53x18x35	126
CA48	GFC	Y	Y	Y	Y	Y		Y		Y		1	5/5	53x18x35	126
CA58	GFC	Y	Y	Y	Y	Y		Y	USB	Y	Y	2	5/5	57x18x36	161
CA58	GFC	Y	Y	Y	Y	Y		Y	USB	Y	Y	2	5/5	57x18x36	161
CA78	GFII	Y	Y	Y	Y	Y		Y	USB	Y	Y	2	5/5	57x18x36	163
CA78	GFII	Y	Y	Y	Y	Y		Y	USB	Y	Y	2	5/5	57x18x36	163
CA78	GFII	Y	Y	Y	Y	Y		Y	USB	Y	Y	2	5/5	57x18x36	163
CA98	GFII	Y	Y	Y	Y	Y		Y	USB	Y	Y	2	5/5	57x18x37	187
CA98	GFII	Y	Y	Y	Y	Y		Y	USB	Y	Y	2	5/5	57x18x37	187
CA98	GFII	Y	Y	Y	Y	Y		Y	USB	Y	Y	2	5/5	57x18x37	187

Brand & Model	Form	Ensemble	Finish	Estimated Price	MSRP	Sound Source	Voices	Key Off	Sustain	String Resonance	Rhythms/Styles	Polyphony	Total Watts	Speakers	Piano Pedals	Half Pedal
Kawai (continued)																
CS8	V		EP	4,627	5,699	s	60	Y	Y	Y	100	256	100	4	3	Y
CS11	V		EP	6,627	8,499	S	80	Y	Y	Y	100	256	135	6	3	Y
CP3	V	E	R	4,445	5,999	S	700+	Y	Y	Y	215	256	100	2	3	Y
CP3	V	E	ES	4,536	6,099	S	700+	Y	Y	Y	215	256	100	2	3	Y
CP2	V	E	R	5,900	8,999	S	1000+	Y	Y	Y	425	256	100	4	3	Y
CP2	V	E	ES	5,991	9,199	S	1000+	Y	Y	Y	425	256	100	4	3	Y
CP1	G	E	EP	15,173	21,999	S	1000+	Y	Y	Y	425	256	200	9	3	Y
NV10	G		EP	12,995	15,999	M/S	88	Y	Y	Y	100	256	135	7	3	Y
Korg																
B1	S		Bk/Wt	500	700	S	8		Y	Y		120	9	2	1	
SP280	S		Bk/Wt	700	980	S	30					120	44	2	1	Y
SV-1-88	S		Bk	1,750	2,380	S	36		Y	Y		80	0	0	1 (3)	Y
D1	S		Bk	600	840	S	30	Y	Y	Y		120	0	0	1	Y
LP180	V		Bk/Wt	600	980	S	10					120	11	2	3	Y
LP380	V		Bk/Wt/R	1,099	1,399	S	30					120	44	2	3	Y
B1SP	V		Bk/Wt	600	850	S	8		Y	Y		120	9	2	3	
G1 Air	V		Bk/Wt/R	1,599	2,199	S	32	Y	Y	Y		120	80	4	3	Y
C1 Air	V		Bk/Wt/R	1,399	1,699	S	30	Y	Y	Y		120	50	2	3	Y
Kurzweil																
MPS-10	S		Bk	699	999	S	88	Y	Y		78	64	30	2	1	
KA-90	S	E	Bk	599	699	S	20		Y		50	128	60	4	1	
CUP-1	V		EP	2,999	3,999	S	1	Y	Y	Y		256	100	4	3	Y
CUP-2	V		R	2,999	4,499	S	88	Y	Y		78	64	140	4	3	
CUP-320	V		R	2,499	3,999	S	88	Y	Y	Y	69	128	50	4	3	Y
MP-20	V		EP	1,999	2,999	S	200	Y	Y		100	64	45	4	3	Y
MP-20F	V		R	1,999	3,499	S	200	Y	Y		100	64	45	4	3	Y
MP-20F	V		EP	2,499	3,999	S	200	Y	Y		100	64	45	4	3	Y

Kawai *(continued)*

Brand & Model	Action	Triple-Sensor Keys	Escapement	Wood Keys	Ivory Texture	Bluetooth	Vocal Support	Educational Features	External Storage	USB to Computer	USB Digital Audio	Recording Tracks	Warranty (Parts/Labor)	Dimensions WxDxH (Inches)	Weight (Pounds)
CS8	GFII	Y	Y	Y	Y			Y	USB	Y	Y	2	5/5	57x19x37	187
CS11	GFII	Y	Y	Y	Y			Y	USB	Y	Y	2	5/5	60x21x41	218
CP3	RHII	Y	Y		Y			Y	USB	Y	Y	16	5/5	56x23x38	146
CP3	RHII	Y	Y		Y			Y	USB	Y	Y	16	5/5	56x23x38	146
CP2	GF	Y	Y	Y	Y	Y		Y	USB	Y	Y	16	5/5	56x23x38	190
CP2	GF	Y	Y	Y	Y	Y		Y	USB	Y	Y	16	5/5	56x23x38	190
CP1	GF	Y	Y	Y	Y	Y		Y	USB	Y	Y	16	5/5	57x63x39	430
NV10	Millennium III	Y	Y	Y	Y	Y		Y	USB	Y	Y	2	5/5	58x25x36	279

Korg

Brand & Model	Action	Triple-Sensor Keys	Escapement	Wood Keys	Ivory Texture	Bluetooth	Vocal Support	Educational Features	External Storage	USB to Computer	USB Digital Audio	Recording Tracks	Warranty (Parts/Labor)	Dimensions WxDxH (Inches)	Weight (Pounds)
B1	NH						Y					0	1/1	52x14x5	27
SP280	NH											0	1/1	54x16x31	42
SV-1-88	RH3									Y		0	1/1	53x14x6	45
D1	RH3											0	1/1	53x11x5	36
LP180	NH											0	1/1	54x11x31	51
LP380	RH3						Y					0	5/5	53x14x30	82
B1SP	NH						Y					0	1/1	52x14x30	45
G1 Air	RH3					Y	Y			Y		2	5/5	53x15x33	91
C1 Air	RH3					Y	Y			Y		2	5/5	53x14x31	78

Kurzweil

Brand & Model	Action	Triple-Sensor Keys	Escapement	Wood Keys	Ivory Texture	Bluetooth	Vocal Support	Educational Features	External Storage	USB to Computer	USB Digital Audio	Recording Tracks	Warranty (Parts/Labor)	Dimensions WxDxH (Inches)	Weight (Pounds)
MPS-10	Weighted/LK									Y		1	3/2	51x14x4	40
KA-90	Weighted									Y		1	3/2	54x14x5	27
CUP-1	Weighted, graded			Y	Y					Y	Y	0	3/2	56x17x42	221
CUP-2	Weighted, graded	Y	Y							Y		1	3/2	56x17x42	214
CUP-320	Weighted, graded	Y		Y				Y		Y		1	3/2	56x19x35	105
MP-20	Weighted, graded/LK	Y								Y		2	3/2	55x20x35	156
MP-20F	Weighted, graded/Fatar	Y								Y		2	3/2	55x20x35	156
MP-20F	Weighted, graded/Fatar	Y								Y		2	3/2	55x20x35	156

Kurzweil (continued)

Brand & Model	Form	Ensemble	Finish	Estimated Price	MSRP	Sound Source	Voices	Key Off	Sustain	String Resonance	Rhythms/Styles	Polyphony	Total Watts	Speakers	Piano Pedals	Half Pedal
KAG-100	G	E	EP	2,499	3,999	S	200		Y		100	64	35	4	3	
MPG-100	G	E	EP	3,999	5,999	S	500		Y		200	128	60	4	3	Y

Nord

Brand & Model	Form	Ensemble	Finish	Estimated Price	MSRP	Sound Source	Voices	Key Off	Sustain	String Resonance	Rhythms/Styles	Polyphony	Total Watts	Speakers	Piano Pedals	Half Pedal
Nord Piano 3	S		Rd	2,699	3,399	S	1000+		Y	Y		40-60	0	0	3	Y
Nord Piano 4	S		Rd	2,999		S	1000+		Y	Y		120	0	0	3	Y

Physis

Brand & Model	Form	Ensemble	Finish	Estimated Price	MSRP	Sound Source	Voices	Key Off	Sustain	String Resonance	Rhythms/Styles	Polyphony	Total Watts	Speakers	Piano Pedals	Half Pedal
H1	S		Alu	2,995	4,995	M	192	Y	Y	Y		UL	0	0	3	Y
H2	S		Alu	2,295	4,295	M	192	Y	Y	Y		UL	0	0	3	Y
K4EX	S		Bl	2,640	3,795	M	192	Y	Y	Y		UL	0	0	3	Y
V100	V		PE/PRd/PWt/SG/PBl	6,899	9,695	M	192	Y	Y	Y		UL	150	6	3	Y
G1000	G		EP			M	192	Y	Y	Y		UL	160	6	3	Y

Roland

Brand & Model	Form	Ensemble	Finish	Estimated Price	MSRP	Sound Source	Voices	Key Off	Sustain	String Resonance	Rhythms/Styles	Polyphony	Total Watts	Speakers	Piano Pedals	Half Pedal
RD-2000	S		Bk	2,499	2,999	M/S	1100+	Y	Y	Y	200	UL/128	0	0	1 (3)	Y
V-Piano	S		Bk	6,999	7,999	M	24	Y	Y	Y		264	0	0	3	Y
GO:PIANO88	S		Bk	399	399	s	4		Y			128	20	2	1	
FP-10	S		Bk	499	649	M/S	15	Y	Y	Y		96	12	2	1	Y
FP-10C	V		Bk	589	779	M/S	15	Y	Y	Y		96	12	2	1	Y
FP-30	S	E	Bk/Wt	699	899	M/S	35	Y	Y	Y	8	128	22	2	1 (3)	
FP-30C	V	E	Bk/Wt	899	1,119	M/S	35	Y	Y	Y	8	128	22	2	3	Y
FP-60	S	E	Bk/Wt	1,459	1,799	M/S	355	Y	Y	Y	21	288	26	2	1 (3)	Y
FP-60C	V	E	Bk/Wt	1,799	2,299	M/S	355	Y	Y	Y	21	288	26	2	3	Y
FP-90	S	E	Bk/Wt	1,899	2,299	M	355	Y	Y	Y	21	UL/384	60	4	1 (3)	Y
FP-90C	V	E	Bk/Wt	2,299	2,799	M	355	Y	Y	Y	21	UL/384	60	4	3	Y
DP-603	V	E	Bk	2,499	2,999	M	319	Y	Y	Y	21	UL/384	24	2	3	Y
DP-603	V	E	EP/WtP	3,099	3,699	M	319	Y	Y	Y	21	UL/384	24	2	3	Y
HP-504	V		R/ES	2,199	2,499	M/S	350	Y	Y	Y		128	24	2	3	Y
HP-601	V	E	R/ES/Wt	2,299	2,799	M/S	319	Y	Y	Y	21	288	28	2	3	Y

Brand & Model	Action	Triple-Sensor Keys	Escapement	Wood Keys	Ivory Texture	Bluetooth	Vocal Support	Educational Features	External Storage	USB to Computer	USB Digital Audio	Recording Tracks	Warranty (Parts/Labor)	Dimensions WxDxH (Inches)	Weight (Pounds)
Kurzweil *(continued)*															
KAG-100	Weighted					Y		Y	USB	Y	Y	2	3/2	56x30x35	150
MPG-100	Weighted, graded	Y					Y			Y		6	3/2	56x36x35	212
Nord															
Nord Piano 3	Fatar Weighted	Y								Y		0	1/1	51x13x5	40
Nord Piano 4	Fatar Weighted	Y								Y		0	1/1	51x13x5	40
Physis															
H1	Tri-sensor, Hybrid	Y	Y	Y	Y				USB	Y	Y	16	3/1	54x13x4	58
H2	Lightweight Hammer, 3 sensors	Y	Y						USB	Y	Y	16	3/1	54x13x4	45
K4EX	Tri-sensor, Hybrid	Y	Y						USB	Y	Y	16	3/1	51x14x5	40
V100	Tri-sensor, Hybrid	Y	Y	Y	Y				USB	Y	Y	16	3/1	58x17x46	233
G1000	Tri-sensor, Hybrid	Y	Y	Y	Y				USB	Y		2	3/1	57x40x56	288
Roland															
RD-2000	PHA-50 Concert	Y	Y	Y	Y				USB	Y	Y	1	3/2	56x15x6	55
V-Piano	PHA III	Y	Y	Y					USB	Y	Y	0	3/2	56x21x7	84
GO:PIANO88	Touch Sensitive					Y	Y		Y				1/90	51x11x5	16
FP-10	PHA-4 Standard	Y	Y		Y		Y		Y				3/2	51x11x6	27
FP-10C	PHA-4 Standard	Y	Y		Y	Y	Y		Y				3/2	51x13x36	44
FP-30	PHA-4 Standard	Y	Y		Y		Y		USB	Y	Y	1	5/2	51x11x6	31
FP-30C	PHA-4 Standard	Y	Y		Y	Y	Y		USB	Y	Y	1	5/2	51x13x36	57
FP-60	PHA-4 Standard	Y	Y		Y	Y	Y		USB	Y	Y	1	5/2	51x14x5	42
FP-60C	PHA-4 Standard	Y	Y		Y	Y	Y		USB	Y	Y	1	5/2	51x14x37	72
FP-90	PHA-50 Concert	Y	Y	Y	Y	Y	Y	Y	USB	Y	Y	2	5/2	53x15x5	52
FP-90C	PHA-50 Concert	Y	Y	Y	Y	Y	Y	Y	USB	Y	Y	2	5/2	53x15x37	83
DP-603	PHA-50 Concert	Y	Y	Y	Y	Y		Y	USB	Y	Y	3	5/2	55x14x31	104
DP-603	PHA-50 Concert	Y	Y	Y	Y	Y		Y	USB	Y	Y	3	5/2	55x14x31	104
HP-504	PHA4-Premium	Y	Y		Y			Y	USB	Y	Y	3	5/2	55x17x41	114
HP-601	PHA-50 Concert	Y	Y	Y	Y	Y		Y	USB	Y	Y	3	5/2	54x17x40	110

Digital Piano Specifications & Prices

Roland (continued)

Brand & Model	Form	Ensemble	Finish	Estimated Price	MSRP	Sound Source	Voices	Key Off	Sustain	String Resonance	Rhythms/Styles	Polyphony	Total Watts	Speakers	Piano Pedals	Half Pedal
HP-603	V	E	R/ES/Wt	2,999	3,399	M	319	Y	Y	Y	21	UL/384	60	2	3	Y
HP-603A	V	E	R/ES/Wt	3,199	3,499	M	319	Y	Y	Y	21	UL/384	60	2	3	Y
HP-605	V	E	EP	4,349	4,999	M	319	Y	Y	Y	21	UL/384	74	6	3	Y
HP-605	V	E	R/ES/Wt	3,849	4,499	M	319	Y	Y	Y	21	UL/384	74	6	3	Y
HPi-50e	V	E	R	4,499	4,999	M/S	350	Y	Y	Y	50	128	74	4	3	Y
LX-7	V	E	EP	5,499	6,299	M	319	Y	Y	Y	21	UL/384	74	6	3	Y
LX-7	V	E	W/ES	5,999	6,899	M	319	Y	Y	Y	21	UL/384	74	6	3	Y
LX-17	V	E	EP	6,499	7,599	M	319	Y	Y	Y	21	UL/384	74	8	3	Y
LX-17	V	E	WtP	6,799	7,999	M	319	Y	Y	Y	21	UL/384	74	8	3	Y
LX-705	V	E	O/R/ES	3,799	4,299	M	324	Y	Y	Y	21	UL/256	60	4	3	Y
LX-705	V	E	EP	4,299	4,799	M	324	Y	Y	Y	21	UL/256	60	4	3	Y
LX-706	V	E	R/ES	4,999	5,599	M	324	Y	Y	Y	21	UL/256	74	6	3	Y
LX-706	V	E	EP	5,599	6,199	M	324	Y	Y	Y	21	UL/256	74	6	3	Y
LX-708	V	E	ES	5,999	6,699	M	324	Y	Y	Y	21	UL/256	74	8	3	Y
LX-708	V	E	EP	6,699	7,399	M	324	Y	Y	Y	21	UL/256	74	8	3	Y
LX-708	V	E	WtP	6,999	7,699	M	324	Y	Y	Y	21	UL/256	74	8	3	Y
F-140R	V	E	ES/Wt	1,249	1,499	M/S	316	Y	Y	Y	72	128	24	2	3	Y
RP-102	V	E	Bk	999	1,199	M/S	318	Y	Y	Y	21	128	12	2	3	Y
RP-501R	V	E	Bk/Wt/R	1,599	1,999	M/S	316	Y	Y	Y	72	128	24	2	3	Y
GP-7 (V-Piano Grand)	G		EP	19,950	22,999	M	30	Y	Y	Y		264	240	8	3	Y
GP-607 (Mini Grand)	G	E	EP	6,199	7,699	M	319	Y	Y	Y	21	UL/384	70	5	3	Y
GP-607 (Mini Grand)	G	E	WtP	6,499	7,999	M	319	Y	Y	Y	21	UL/384	70	5	3	Y
GP-609 (Grand Piano)	G	E	EP	9,399	10,699	M	319	Y	Y	Y	21	UL/384	74	7	3	Y
GP-609 (Grand Piano)	G	E	WtP	9,899	11,399	M	319	Y	Y	Y	21	UL/384	74	7	3	Y

Samick

Brand & Model	Form	Ensemble	Finish	Estimated Price	MSRP	Sound Source	Voices	Key Off	Sustain	String Resonance	Rhythms/Styles	Polyphony	Total Watts	Speakers	Piano Pedals	Half Pedal
Ebony NEO	V		EP	4,089	4,095	S	10	Y	Y	Y		135	80	4	3	Y
SG-120	G	E	EP/WtP/RdP	3,907	4,295	S	377	Y	Y	Y	353	128	60	6	3	Y
SG-500	G	E	EP/WtP/RdP	4,816	5,295	S	377	Y	Y	Y	352	128	80	8	3	Y

Brand & Model	Action	Triple-Sensor Keys	Escapement	Wood Keys	Ivory Texture	Bluetooth	Vocal Support	Educational Features	External Storage	USB to Computer	USB Digital Audio	Recording Tracks	Warranty (Parts/Labor)	Dimensions WxDxH (Inches)	Weight (Pounds)
Roland (continued)															
HP-603	PHA-50 Concert	Y	Y	Y	Y	Y		Y	USB	Y	Y	3	10/10	54x17x42	110
HP-603A	PHA-50 Concert	Y	Y	Y	Y	Y		Y	USB	Y	Y	3	10/10	54x17x42	110
HP-605	PHA-50 Concert	Y	Y	Y	Y	Y		Y	USB	Y	Y	3	10/10	54x17x44	119
HP-605	PHA-50 Concert	Y	Y	Y	Y	Y		Y	USB	Y	Y	3	10/10	54x17x44	119
HPi-50e	PHA4-Concert	Y	Y		Y			Y	USB	Y	Y	16	5/2	55x17x43	127
LX-7	PHA-50 Concert	Y	Y	Y	Y	Y		Y	USB	Y	Y	3	10/10	55x18x41	170
LX-7	PHA-50 Concert	Y	Y	Y	Y	Y		Y	USB	Y	Y	3	10/10	55x18x41	170
LX-17	PHA-50 Concert	Y	Y	Y	Y	Y			USB	Y	Y	3	10/10	55x19x42	193
LX-17	PHA-50 Concert	Y	Y	Y	Y	Y			USB	Y	Y	3	10/10	55x19x42	193
LX-705	PHA-50 Concert	Y	Y	Y	Y	Y		Y	USB	Y	Y	3	10/10	54x18x41	164
LX-705	PHA-50 Concert	Y	Y	Y	Y	Y		Y	USB	Y	Y	3	10/10	54x18x41	167
LX-706	PHA-100 Hybrid Grand	Y	Y	Y	Y	Y		Y	USB	Y	Y	3	10/10	54x19x44	212
LX-706	PHA-100 Hybrid Grand	Y	Y	Y	Y	Y		Y	USB	Y	Y	3	10/10	54x19x44	216
LX-708	PHA-100 Hybrid Grand	Y	Y	Y	Y	Y		Y	USB	Y	Y	3	10/10	55x19x46	240
LX-708	PHA-100 Hybrid Grand	Y	Y	Y	Y	Y		Y	USB	Y	Y	3	10/10	55x19x46	243
LX-708	PHA-100 Hybrid Grand	Y	Y	Y	Y	Y		Y	USB	Y	Y	3	10/10	55x19x46	243
F-140R	PHA-4-Standard	Y	Y		Y	Y		Y	USB	Y	Y	1	5/2	54x14x31	76
RP-102	PHA4-Standard	Y	Y		Y	Y		Y		Y			5/2	54x17x39	83
RP-501R	PHA-4 Standard	Y	Y		Y	Y		Y	USB	Y	Y	1	5/2	54x12x31	81
GP-7 (V-Piano Grand)	PHA III	Y	Y		Y				USB	Y	Y	1	5/2	59x59x61	375
GP-607 (Mini Grand)	PHA-50 Concert	Y	Y	Y	Y	Y		Y	USB	Y	Y	3	10/10	55x37x35	223
GP-607 (Mini Grand)	PHA-50 Concert	Y	Y	Y	Y	Y		Y	USB	Y	Y	3	10/10	55x37x35	223
GP-609 (Grand Piano)	PHA-50 Concert	Y	Y	Y	Y	Y		Y	USB	Y	Y	3	10/10	57x59x62	326
GP-609 (Grand Piano)	PHA-50 Concert	Y	Y	Y	Y	Y		Y	USB	Y	Y	3	10/10	57x59x62	326
Samick															
Ebony NEO	Graded	Y			Y	Y	Y	Y	USB	Y	Y	2	3/3	57x19x41	170
SG-120	Graded	Y			Y	Y	Y	Y	USB	Y	Y	5	3/3	56x35x29	170
SG-500	Graded	Y			Y	Y	Y	Y	USB	Y	Y	5	3/3	56x49x35	290

Digital Piano Specifications & Prices

Brand & Model	Form	Ensemble	Finish	Estimated Price	MSRP	Sound Source	Voices	Key Off	Sustain	String Resonance	Rhythms/Styles	Polyphony	Total Watts	Speakers	Piano Pedals	Half Pedal
Suzuki																
SCP-88	V		Bk	899	1,099	S	24					128	30	2	3	
VG-88	V		R	1,599		S	16+128GM	Y	Y			189	40	4	3	
CTP-88	V	E	M	999	1,200	S	122+128GM	Y	Y		100	128	60	4	3	
SDP-2000ts	V	E	R	1,299		S	672+256GM				240	128	220	4	3	
MDG-300	G	E	EP	1,699	3,390	S	122+128GM	Y	Y		100	128	120	6	3	
MDG-330	G	E	EP	2,299	3,500	S	122+128GM	Y	Y		100	128	120	6	3	
MDG-400	G		EP	2,699	4,200	S	122+128GM	Y	Y		100	128	120	6	3	
MDG-4000ts	G		EP	3,399	5,899	S	672+256GM				240	128	250	6	3	
Williams																
Legato III	S		Bk	199	229	S	10		Y			64	40	2	1	
Allegro III	S		Bk	299	329	S	10		Y			64	60	2	1	
Rhapsody 2	V		WG/EP	499	900	S	12		Y			64	60	2	2	
Overture 2	V		EP/RdM	699	1,200	S	19+128GM		Y			64	60	4	3	
Symphony Grand	G	E	EP/RdM	1,499	1,999	S	46+128GM	Y	Y	Y	120	128	60	6		
Yamaha																
P45B	S		Bk	450	499	S	10					64	12	2	1	Y
P125	S		Bk/Wt	600	999	S	24			20		192	14	4	1 (3)	Y
P255	S		Bk&EP/Wt	1,300	1,999	S	24	Y	Y	Y	10	256	30	4	1	Y
P515	S		Bk/Wt	1,499	1,999	S	40+480XG	Y	Y	Y	40	256	40	4	1 (3)	Y
CP300	S		Bk	2,500	3,499	S	50+480XG	Y	Y	Y		128	60	2	3	Y
CP40 Stage	S		Bk	1,400	2,399	M/S	297	Y	Y			128	0	0	1 (2)	Y
CP4 Stage	S		Bk	2,000	2,699	M/S	433	Y	Y			128	0	0	1 (2)	Y
CP1	S		Bk	5,000	5,999	M/S	17	Y	Y	Y		128	0	0	3	Y
YDP143	V		BkW/R	1,100	1,499	S	10					192	12	2	3	Y
YDP144	V		BkW/R	1,100	1,499	S	10					192	12	2	3	Y
YDPS34	V		BkW/R	1,100	1,399	S	10					192	12	2	3	Y

Suzuki

Brand & Model	Action	Triple-Sensor Keys	Escapement	Wood Keys	Ivory Texture	Bluetooth	Vocal Support	Educational Features	External Storage	USB to Computer	USB Digital Audio	Recording Tracks	Warranty (Parts/Labor)	Dimensions WxDxH (Inches)	Weight (Pounds)
SCP-88	Weighted									Y		0	1/1	54x18x34	
VG-88	Graded					Y	Y			Y		1	1/1	58x19x41	236
CTP-88	Graded						Y		SD	Y		3	1/1	54x20x40	175
SDP-2000ts	Graded						Y		SD	Y		16	1/1	55x24x36	152
MDG-300	Graded						Y		SD	Y		3	1/1	55x30x36	218
MDG-330	Graded						Y		SD	Y		3	1/1	57x39x36	330
MDG-400	Graded						Y		SD	Y		3	1/1	55x49x35	315
MDG-4000ts	Fatar Graded						Y		SD	Y		16	1/1	58x48x37	311

Williams

Brand & Model	Action	Triple-Sensor Keys	Escapement	Wood Keys	Ivory Texture	Bluetooth	Vocal Support	Educational Features	External Storage	USB to Computer	USB Digital Audio	Recording Tracks	Warranty (Parts/Labor)	Dimensions WxDxH (Inches)	Weight (Pounds)
Legato III	Semi-Weighted					Y		Y		Y		0	1/1	50x11x4	19
Allegro III	Weighted					Y		Y		Y		1	1/1	52x5x13	30
Rhapsody 2	Weighted									Y		2	1/1	54x16x31	83
Overture 2	Weighted							Y	USB	Y		2	1/1	55x19x34	117
Symphony Grand	Graded, Weighted					Y		Y	USB	Y	Y	4	1/1	54x35x36	163

Yamaha

Brand & Model	Action	Triple-Sensor Keys	Escapement	Wood Keys	Ivory Texture	Bluetooth	Vocal Support	Educational Features	External Storage	USB to Computer	USB Digital Audio	Recording Tracks	Warranty (Parts/Labor)	Dimensions WxDxH (Inches)	Weight (Pounds)
P45B	GHS									Y		0	3/3	52x12x6	26
P125	GHS									Y	Y	2	3/3	52x12x6	26
P255	GH			Y					USB	Y	Y	2	3/3	53x14x6	38
P515	NWX	Y	Y	Y	Y	Y			USB	Y	Y	16	3/3	53x14x7	48
CP300	GH									Y		16	3/3	54x18x7	72
CP40 Stage	GH								USB	Y	Y	0	3/3	52x14x6	36
CP4 Stage	NW-GH3	Y		Y	Y				USB	Y	Y	0	3/3	52x14x6	39
CP1	NW-Stage			Y	Y				USB	Y		0	3/3	55x17x7	60
YDP143	GHS									Y		2	3/3	54x17x32	84
YDP144	GHS									Y	Y	2	3/3	54x17x33	84
YDPS34	GHS									Y	Y	2	3/3	54x17x31	80

Yamaha (continued)

Brand & Model	Form	Ensemble	Finish	Estimated Price	MSRP	Sound Source	Voices	Key Off	Sustain	String Resonance	Rhythms/Styles	Polyphony	Total Watts	Speakers	Piano Pedals	Half Pedal
YDP163	V		BkW/R	1,500	1,999	S	10					192	40	4	3	Y
YDP164	V		BkW/R	1,500	1,999	S	10					192	40	4	3	Y
YDPS52	V		Bk/Wt	1,350	2,199	S	10					192	40	2	3	Y
YDPS54	V		Bk/Wt	1,350	2,199	S	10					192	40	4	3	Y
YDP181	V		R	1,700	2,199	S	14					128	40	2	3	Y
YDP184	V		R	2,200	2,799	S	24	Y	Y	Y		256	60	2	3	Y
CSP150	V	E	Bk	3,500	3,999	S	721+480XG	Y	Y	Y	470	256	60	2	3	Y
CSP150	V	E	EP	4,000	4,599	S	721+480XG	Y	Y	Y	470	256	60	2	3	Y
CSP170	V	E	Bk	4,700	5,399	S	721+480XG	Y	Y	Y	470	256	180	4	3	Y
CSP170	V	E	EP	5,300	5,999	S	721+480XG	Y	Y	Y	470	256	180	4	3	Y
CLP625	V		EP	2,400	2,699	S	10	Y	Y	Y		256	40	2	3	Y
CLP625	V		Bk/R	2,000	2,299	S	10	Y	Y	Y		256	40	2	3	Y
CLP635	V		EP	3,200	3,599	S	36	Y	Y	Y	20	256	60	2	3	Y
CLP635	V		Bk/R/W	2,700	2,999	S	36	Y	Y	Y	20	256	60	2	3	Y
CLP645	V		EP	4,000	4,599	S	36	Y	Y	Y	20	256	100	4	3	Y
CLP645	V		Bk/R/W	3,500	3,999	S	36	Y	Y	Y	20	256	100	4	3	Y
CLP675	V		EP	5,300	5,999	S	36	Y	Y	Y	20	256	210	6	3	Y
CLP675	V		BK/R/W	4,700	5,199	S	36	Y	Y	Y	20	256	210	6	3	Y
CLP685	V		EP	6,600	7,499	S	49+480XG	Y	Y	Y	20	256	300	6	3	Y
CLP685	V		WtP	7,600	8,474	S	49+480XG	Y	Y	Y	20	256	300	6	3	Y
CLP685	V		Bk	5,800	6,499	S	49+480XG	Y	Y	Y	20	256	300	6	3	Y
CVP701	V	E	W	4,127	5,399	S	777+480XG	Y	Y	Y	310	256	50	2	3	Y
CVP701	V	E	EP	4,636	6,199	S	777+480XG	Y	Y	Y	310	256	50	2	3	Y
CVP705	V	E	W	6,455	8,699	S	984+480XG	Y	Y	Y	470	256	140	6	3	Y
CVP705	V	E	EP	7,245	9,699	S	984+480XG	Y	Y	Y	470	256	140	6	3	Y
CVP709	V	E	W	10,091	14,499	S	1270+480XG	Y	Y	Y	600	256	200	9	3	Y
CVP709	V	E	EP	11,087	15,999	S	1270+480XG	Y	Y	Y	600	256	200	9	3	Y
NU1X	V		EP	5,907	6,999	S	15	Y	Y	Y		256	180	4	3	Y

Brand & Model	Action	Triple-Sensor Keys	Escapement	Wood Keys	Ivory Texture	Bluetooth	Vocal Support	Educational Features	External Storage	USB to Computer	USB Digital Audio	Recording Tracks	Warranty (Parts/Labor)	Dimensions WxDxH (Inches)	Weight (Pounds)
Yamaha *(continued)*															
YDP163	GH3	Y			Y					Y		2	3/3	54x17x33	93
YDP164	GH3	Y			Y					Y	Y	2	3/3	54x17x34	93
YDPS52	GH				Y					Y		2	3/3	55x12x31	80
YDPS54	GH3	Y			Y					Y	Y	2	3/3	55x12x31	80
YDP181	GH								USB	Y		2	3/3	54x34x20	110
YDP184	GH3	Y			Y				USB	Y		16	3/3	57x36x18	123
CSP150	GH3X	Y	Y		Y		Y	Y	USB-Tablet	Y	Y	16	5/5	56x18x40	127
CSP150	GH3X	Y	Y		Y		Y	Y	USB-Tablet	Y	Y	17	5/6	56x18x40	127
CSP170	NWX	Y	Y	Y	Y		Y	Y	USB-Tablet	Y	Y	18	5/7	56x18x40	147
CSP170	NWX	Y	Y	Y	Y		Y	Y	USB-Tablet	Y	Y	19	5/8	56x18x40	147
CLP625	GH3X	Y	Y		Y					Y		2	5/5	53x16x33	95
CLP625	GH3X	Y	Y		Y					Y		2	5/5	53x16x33	99
CLP635	GH3X	Y	Y		Y			Y	USB	Y	Y	16	5/5	58x18x37	123
CLP635	GH3X	Y	Y		Y			Y	USB	Y	Y	16	5/5	58x18x37	137
CLP645	NWX	Y	Y	Y	Y	Y		Y	USB	Y	Y	16	5/5	58x18x37	132
CLP645	NWX	Y	Y	Y	Y	Y		Y	USB	Y	Y	16	5/5	58x18x37	146
CLP675	GrandTouch	Y	Y	Y	Y	Y		Y	USB	Y	Y	16	5/5	58x19x38	152
CLP675	GrandTouch	Y	Y	Y	Y	Y		Y	USB	Y	Y	16	5/5	58x19x38	157
CLP685	GrandTouch	Y	Y	Y	Y	Y		Y	USB	Y	Y	16	5/5	58x19x41	183
CLP685	GrandTouch	Y	Y	Y	Y	Y		Y	USB	Y	Y	16	5/5	58x19x41	183
CLP685	GrandTouch	Y	Y	Y	Y	Y		Y	USB	Y	Y	16	5/5	58x19x41	196
CVP701	GH3X		Y		Y		Y	Y	USB	Y	Y	16	5/5	53x24x36	130
CVP701	GH3X	Y	Y		Y		Y	Y	USB	Y	Y	16	5/5	53x24x36	130
CVP705	NWX	Y	Y	Y	Y		Y	Y	USB	Y	Y	16	5/5	56x24x34	170
CVP705	NWX	Y	Y	Y	Y		Y	Y	USB	Y	Y	16	5/5	56x24x34	170
CVP709	NWX	Y	Y	Y	Y		Y	Y	USB	Y	Y	16	5/5	56x24x34	174
CVP709	NWX	Y	Y	Y	Y		Y	Y	USB	Y	Y	16	5/5	56x24x34	174
NU1X	Specialized Upright			Y		Y			USB	Y	Y	1	5/5	60x18x40	240

Digital Piano Specifications & Prices

Brand & Model	Form	Ensemble	Finish	Estimated Price	MSRP	Sound Source	Voices	Key Off	Sustain	String Resonance	Rhythms/Styles	Polyphony	Total Watts	Speakers	Piano Pedals	Half Pedal
Yamaha (continued)																
NU1X	V		WtP	6,180	7,199	S	15	Y	Y	Y		256	180	4	3	Y
N1X	G		EP	8,999	10,999	S	15	Y	Y	Y		256	180	6	3	Y
N2	G		EP	12,635	14,999	S	5	Y	Y	Y		256	500	12	3	Y
N3X	G		EP	18,816	22,199	S	10	Y	Y	Y		256	500	12	3	Y
CLP665GP	G		EP	5,500	6,199	S	36	Y	Y	Y	20	256	70	4	3	Y
CLP665GP	G		WtP	6,300	6,999	S	36	Y	Y	Y	20	256	70	4	3	Y
CVP709GP	G	E	EP	15,224	20,999	S	1270+ 480XG	Y	Y	Y	600	256	200	9	3	Y

Yamaha (continued)

Brand & Model	Action	Triple-Sensor Keys	Escapement	Wood Keys	Ivory Texture	Bluetooth	Vocal Support	Educational Features	External Storage	USB to Computer	USB Digital Audio	Recording Tracks	Warranty (Parts/Labor)	Dimensions WxDxH (Inches)	Weight (Pounds)
NU1X	Specialized Upright			Y		Y			USB	Y	Y	1	5/5	60x18x40	240
N1X	Specialized Grand		Y	Y		Y			USB	Y	Y	1	5/5	58x24x39	257
N2	Specialized Grand		Y	Y	Y				USB			1	5/5	58x21x40	313
N3X	Specialized Grand		Y	Y	Y				USB	Y	Y	1	5/5	58x47x40	439
CLP665GP	GH3X	Y	Y		Y	Y		Y	USB	Y	Y	16	1	56x45x37	227
CLP665GP	GH3X	Y	Y		Y	Y		Y	USB	Y	Y	16	1	56x45x37	227
CVP709GP	NWX	Y	Y	Y	Y		Y	Y	USB	Y	Y	16	5/5	56x45x36	242